a little
bit funny

Aurum Press

THANKS

This life owes a lot to other lives, notably Ian Birrell, Johnny Dee, Adrian Deevoy, Peter Doggett, Ken Hunt, Phil Kear, Linda Kenis, Andrew King, Kas Mercer and Sue Parr. And for pulling it all together John, Mal and all the Emmas...

The Elton John Story

Patrick Humphries

First published in Great Britain in1998 by

Aurum Press Ltd
25 Bedford Avenue
London WC1B 3AT

A catalogue record for this book is available from the British Library

ISBN 1 85410 582 5

Design: **Neal Townsend** @ **JMP Ltd**
Picture research: **Karen Tucker** @ **JMP Ltd**

Printed and bound in Great Britain by Jarrold Book Printing, Thetford

what a long strange trip it's been

The majority of people have always liked Elton John. They have been with him through nearly thirty years of ups and downs: the hits and the hair transplants, the public showmanship, and the private pain of his ill-fated marriage. Even during the wilderness years of bulimia and the self-confessed sex and drugs nightmares, he was more pitied than reviled. But it was not until the morning of 6 September 1997 that the whole world really came to love Elton John.

When news broke during that extraordinary week that 'Candle In The Wind', one of Elton's best-loved songs, had been re-written by his long-time lyricist Bernie Taupin for the funeral of Diana, Princess of Wales, there was more than a little unease. The original lyrics, about the untimely death of Marilyn Monroe, were particularly scathing about the way Marilyn had been hounded by the press – in death as in life. The comparisons were inescapable, but at the same time they seemed not altogether appropriate. Lyrics written to order are rarely successful, and when Taupin's new words – dashed off in little more than an hour – first

Elton with close friend Princess Diana. His new version of 'Candle In The Wind' articulated the nation's grief at her untimely death

appeared in cold print, they did not look set to be a triumph.

But in the hands of such a consummate pop professional as Elton, 'Candle In The Wind' became both the defining moment of the Princess's funeral and the perfect expression of a whole nation's heartfelt mourning. In a few brief minutes, which to him must have seemed interminable, Elton John became a modern day poet laureate; and in that one performance, he gave voice to the feelings of grief and shared loss, which many had been too shocked and

too numb to articulate.

Even for someone like Elton, who was accustomed to playing before royalty and huge crowds, singing that song at Westminster Abbey must surely have been the most difficult performance of his professional career. Despite being a seasoned performer, Elton – who had known Princess Diana personally – must have found the emotional charge of the funeral service almost overwhelming. There was nowhere to hide, no choir or orchestra for support, no chance of a second take; just his

*Elton John in the early '70s – from a
shy appearance on* Top Of The Pops
to world-stardom

piano, his voice, and the terror of slipping by
force of habit into the familiar old words of a
song he had been singing the same way for
nearly a quarter of a century.

With the eyes of half the world on him, Elton
triumphed. Word perfect, he sang with feeling
but managed to keep the emotion in check until
he had finished his tribute. Suddenly Taupin's
re-written words didn't seem so corny after all,
and Elton had found a place in the hearts of a
nation which had only recently discovered how
much it needed flawed heroes.

As the crow flies, the Abbey is just a few
miles from Pinner in Middlesex. But Reg Dwight

had come by a longer, more interesting route: a
trip which had taken him all around the world,
to unimagined heights of fame and success and
to the very depths of despair. It had been a
turbulent transformation from shy, plump piano
protégé to glamorous, global superstar; a
troubled journey played out over half a century,
most of it in full public view. Elton John has
always been one of the most visible superstars
and, unlike most public lives, in his we have
glimpsed as much pain as partying.

He began, looking young and very nervous,
singing 'Your Song' on *Top Of The Pops* in
January 1971. Within a couple of years, Elton
John had become the most exuberantly over-
the-top pop star rock 'n' roll had ever seen.
Even during that outrageously flamboyant era,
when Glam rock stars like Marc Bolan, Gary
Glitter and David Bowie were teetering around
precariously on platform shoes desperately
trying to out-dress each other, it was usually
Elton whose platforms were the highest; Elton
who could always be relied upon to take
extravagance to extremes.

However consummate the showmanship, it
seemed that Elton's public posturing served only
to emphasise his inner discomfort. He remained
excruciatingly lacking in confidence, while at
the same time the stubborn denial of his own
homosexuality was exacting an ever higher
price on his peace of mind. Before long,

rumours of drug abuse, tales of desperate and painful efforts to replace his rapidly thinning hair, his confessed inability to sustain relationships...all began to play an equally public part in the life and times of Elton John. The willingness to talk about his problems and share the grief of his personal life soon became one of Elton's most endearing characteristics. Other stars may try to conceal their problems for the sake of keeping up appearances, but Elton was only too happy to admit his shortcomings. Sensing the genuine vulnerability beneath his apparently extrovert personality, people – many of whom weren't even fans of his music – took him to their hearts.

Over the years, his audience has followed Elton John every step of the way: gaping open-mouthed at the outrageous costumes; watching him battle constantly with his weight; sympathising as his marriage foundered; sympathising again when his hair transplants failed to take; admiring his stand against the bullying tactics of the *Sun* when he sued them for libel in 1987 and his determination to help sufferers through the Elton John AIDS Foundation ... Like Princess Diana, Elton John has done his growing up, and made his mistakes, very much in public. Part of the reason for people remaining so fond of him is that they feel as if they know the real Elton – they have sung and struggled alongside him, joined in his joys and triumphs, felt his failures and his despair.

In Westminster Abbey on 6 September 1997, all the accumulated emotions came together during Elton's astonishingly moving performance of 'Candle In The Wind'. For years we had shared his grief and now it seemed that he was sharing ours. Nine days later, at Sir George Martin's Music For Montserrat benefit concert, before a capacity crowd of six thousand and in a line-up bursting with the biggest pop names of the past three decades, the reception accorded Elton John as he took the stage of the Royal Albert Hall was overwhelming.

The rewritten 'Candle In The Wind' had taken him straight to No. 1 and was now well on its way to becoming the best-selling single in the history of the UK music industry. The warmth of public affection flooded over the footlights. As he sat down at the piano and picked out the haunting opening chords of his very first hit, 'Your Song', there can have been few amongst the audience who didn't think back to the chubby young singer who had sung the song the first time they heard it. Here tonight was an older and wiser figure, a more commanding presence, and outwardly at least more confident – but still undeniably Elton.

Over the years, Elton's melodies and the accompanying lyrics from Bernie Taupin have combined to make them the most successful pop partnership since Lennon and McCartney. Their songs are inextricably woven into the fabric of the nation's musical memory: 'Your

Goodbye England's Rose – Bernie Taupin's re-written lyric spoke for Britain's sense of loss

Song'; 'Daniel'; 'Rocket Man'; 'Don't Let The Sun Go Down On Me'; 'Sorry Seems To Be The Hardest Word'; 'Sacrifice'... So many, and all so familiar. But of the dozens of hits Elton John has enjoyed since 1971, perhaps the one that stands out as having most enchanted the world is 'Candle In The Wind'.

The song had already been a UK hit twice in the years since 1973 when it was first released on the double album *Goodbye Yellow Brick Road*, and the lyrics had immediately touched a chord in the millions who bought it on the album and as a single. But when Elton sang the new version on that strangely unforgettable day, his poignant performance, the re-written lyrics, the hushed sense of history being made,

all helped propel 'Candle In The Wind' into the very heart of the nation. The crowds in Hyde Park were moved to tears and then to spontaneous applause by Elton's performance. Hearing the new lyrics sung for the first time, perhaps they remembered the original refrain – and how poignant it now seemed.

From fresh-faced pop singer to national icon, all in the course of a quarter of a century. Elton confided to an interviewer not long after, that 'One of the good things about growing older is that you become more honest with yourself.' But in the words of the Grateful Dead, one of the teenage Reg Dwight's favourite bands: 'What a long, strange trip it's been.' **ej**

Blue
Moves

Pinner in Middlesex was first mentioned as a settlement in 1321, and distinguished residents have included a former Governor of Bengal and the comic artist W. Heath Robinson; but it was not until 25 March 1947 that the suburb gained its most famous resident, when Reginald Kenneth Dwight was born in his grandparents' house at 55 Pinner Hill Road.

Stanley Dwight and Sheila Harris met towards the end of World War II. Before the war Stanley had been a milkman, but he joined the RAF as soon as he was old enough, and it

was there that he met Sheila who was working for the RAF as a clerk. They were married in January 1945 and just over two years later their only child was born. The family continued to live with Sheila's parents in Pinner Hill Road for some years after young Reg was born. Stanley Dwight was still serving in the RAF and his duties kept him away from the family home for extended periods, but Sheila doted on young Reg and during the times when Stanley was away, mother and son became very close.

During these very early years Reg also grew

close to his maternal grandmother Ivy and this was a relationship which would remain important to him right up until her death. He always remembered that it was Ivy who had sat him down at the piano at the age of three and made him play. In 1994 when he won an Oscar for 'Can You Feel The Love Tonight', he dedicated the award to his nan who had died just the week before the ceremony.

In later life Elton has had few kind words to say about his father, remembering particularly the pain he felt at overhearing his parents'

frequent furious arguments. Certainly when Stanley was at home, the cosy companionship of mother and son's home life was disturbed by his father's authoritarian nature, and by the time Reg started school he had come to dread the Squadron Leader's sporadic homecomings.

'My father was so stupid with me,' Elton would bitterly recall years later, 'it was ridiculous. I couldn't eat celery without making a noise. It was just pure hate.' Elton's resentment was compounded by his father's refusal to let him wear Hush Puppies and by another occasion when young Reg asked for some of the new rock 'n' roll records which were flooding into 1950s Britain – Stanley Dwight had instead gone out and bought him a record by jazz pianist George Shearing.

From an early age Reg had two abiding loves – music and football – both of which would remain as constants throughout his rollercoaster life. As a young boy, football was the one enthusiasm which he felt able to share with his father. His interest in football was further heightened when a glamorous older cousin, Roy Dwight, secured a place playing for Second Division Fulham FC, although young Reg appreciated that his own chubbiness wasn't going to help him become the next Roy of the Rovers.

One thing at which he did excel was playing the piano and he practised diligently. Before long, music mattered more to Reg Dwight than almost anything else; it became especially important to him because it proved to the world, and to his father, that there was something he could do well – very well. At the age of 11 he won a scholarship to study at the Royal Academy of Music and for the next four years, every Saturday morning, Reg would journey down from Pinner to the Royal Academy's tuition rooms on Marylebone Road, where he took lessons in musical theory, composition and piano.

In 1962 when Reg was 15 years old, Stanley Dwight divorced his wife Sheila on the grounds of her adultery with a local decorator called Fred Farebrother. The marriage had been over in all but name for a long time, but the extended absences caused by Stanley's RAF duties had enabled it to limp on for the sake of appearances. Now though, it was officially over, with Sheila retaining custody of their only child. Once the initial upheaval of the divorce was over, Reg was far happier with his mother and Fred Farebrother. The couple would not marry officially for another ten years, but Fred – or Derf as Reg liked to call him – fell immediately and easily into the role of sympathetic step-father.

An undistinguished student at school, Reg persevered with his weekly piano lessons but made few close friends. He was a solitary teenager who, when he wasn't practising the piano in his bedroom, spent most of the time chronicling the football league tables and weekly pop charts. Later, he would recall the difficulty he had fitting in with his schoolfriends, a lack of acceptance which continued to haunt him long after he became famous: 'I took cocaine and I drank a lot because I felt that might help to loosen me up. I wanted to join the in-crowd. As a kid I was always on the fringe of everything. I wasn't part of the gang. Going out to the cinema with mates, I was always the last one to be asked. I thought that by doing coke I would finally be in with everybody else. And then I got the taste for it.'

During his mid-teens pop increasingly took

Elton – here in his first publicity shot – was inspired to play by his fascination with the Beatles – but he didn't seek to emulate their look

over as Reg's primary interest in life. As a pianist, he was inevitably drawn to the piano-pounding rock 'n' rollers like Little Richard and Jerry Lee Lewis; but his cousin Paul Robinson remembers clearly the 16-year-old's equal enthusiasm for a new group from Liverpool called The Beatles. The young Elton, like so many others, was fascinated by the group's look, but he was also in a position to appreciate the finer points of their intriguing harmonies and melodic poise.

Several years later, at the start of his own professional career, Reg was signed up by Dick James Music; and one of the reasons that this particular signing gave him so much pleasure was that in 1962 the same music publisher had taken a risk on a couple of Liverpudlian

songwriters called Lennon and McCartney. After he became a star in his own right, Elton would enjoy the opportunity to meet 'n' greet the Fab Four on an almost equal footing. And when in 1993 he decided to sell his vast record collection to benefit AIDS charities, Elton is believed to have kept back only two albums: a white-label pressing of a demo session he had recorded with Linda Thompson in 1970, on which they covered songs by Nick Drake, Mike Heron and John Martyn; and his treasured copy of The Beatles' *White Album* on which he had collected separately the autographs of all four Beatles.

In partnership with Bernie Taupin, Elton wrote 'Snookeroo' for Ringo to record and he would get to know both Paul and George; but of the four men, it was John Lennon to whom Elton grew particularly close, after the two met in New York in 1974. For all his reluctance to look back on his Beatle years, Lennon was always keen to meet up with new contenders for the Fab crown. During his nine year exile in New York, between 1971 and his senseless murder in 1980, Lennon grew fond of Elton and also helped out another up and coming Brit called David Bowie.

In 1969 Reg Dwight had won a pair of

*Elton's trademark antics at the piano –
being keyboard-bound has never
meant that he couldn't bop along too*

goldfish and christened them John and Yoko; a few years later, one of Elton John's biggest thrills as a superstar would be his friendship with John Lennon. Elton even became godfather to Sean, Lennon's son with Yoko Ono, and in 1974 played on Lennon's 'Whatever Gets You Thru The Night'. John returned the favour the same year by appearing (under his familiar 'Dr Winston O'Boogie' pseudonym) on 'Lucy In The Sky With Diamonds', Elton's take on the much-loved track from The Beatles' 1967 *Sgt Pepper* album. The resulting single was notable for being the first Elton had ever released which was not written by him and Bernie Taupin.

Convinced that he had a hit on his hands, Elton managed to persuade his Fab collaborator to agree to appear with him on stage, should 'Whatever Gets You Thru The Night' reach No.1 in America. It did, and so on 28 November 1974, John Lennon joined Elton John on-stage at New York's Madison Square Gardens. The crowd went wild. It would prove to be Lennon's final appearance in front of a live audience before his assassination in 1980.

John declined Elton's suggestion to play 'Imagine' and instead performed 'Whatever Gets You Thru The Night', 'Lucy In The Sky With Diamonds' (introduced by Elton as 'one of the best songs ever written') and 'I Saw Her Standing There' – which John told the captivated crowd was by 'an old estranged

fiancé of mine called Paul. This is one I never sang – it's an old Beatle number and we just about know it.' Familiar the song may have been, but that did not make the performance any less nerve-racking. 'We did 'I Saw Her Standing There',' Elton recalled, 'but he never sang it. It was McCartney who sang it. He wanted to go upstairs and be sick. I've never seen anyone so nervous in my life.'

The complete Lennon performance was released in 1995 on the CD single of Elton's 'Made In England': 'It was an unforgettable experience,' Elton said at the time. 'Grown road managers were crying, there was a ten minute ovation and it sends shivers up and down my spine even to think of it now.' With the benefit of hindsight, the evening takes on an even greater poignancy: 'I Saw Her Standing There' had been the opening track on the first-ever album by The Beatles, and now it would prove to be the last song ever performed in public by John Lennon. Following his appearance alongside Elton, Lennon would withdraw to the seclusion of New York's Dakota building to bake bread and bring up Sean. Elton remained a regular visitor though, and following John's assassination he wrote the song 'Empty Garden' in memory of his friend. Like 'Candle In The Wind 1997', this was a song Elton would perform live only once: 'I find it very hard to sing, it upsets me.'

It is unfair and unrealistic to pretend that Elton John was a 1970s answer to The Beatles

– the group's influence was too all-embracing for any subsequent act to fully replicate. But there were definite echoes of the Fabs when, at his peak, Elton John succeeded in reminding the world – and particularly America – just how great can be the impact of a really well-crafted pop song.

As a shy, plump, short-sighted teenager, rock 'n' roll offered Reg Dwight, like so many others who came in on the coat-tails of The Beatles, an opportunity to realise his dreams. Having left school some months before he was due to take his A-Levels, with just four O-Levels to his name – including a surprisingly undistinguished pass in Music – Elton found himself at the age of 18 working as a messenger with Mills Music in London's West End, a position secured for him by his football-playing cousin Roy. By day he would scuttle up and down Denmark Street, the capital's Tin Pan Alley, delivering sheet music, posting parcels and brewing tea. But by night Reg Dwight was busy pursuing his own ambitions.

Within a decade he would be selling out shows at Wembley Stadium and Madison Square Garden, but Elton John's first professional appearances took place in the somewhat humbler surroundings of the Northwood Hills Hotel in Pinner: 'I sang and played piano every Friday, Saturday and Sunday for a whole year. I used to sing Jim Reeves songs, 'When Irish Eyes Are Smiling'. Al Jolson songs were also very popular. I was

earning about £25 a week, which was great.'

The hotel residency led to Reg's first regular gig with a band. Bluesology began in 1965, providing backing for visiting American R&B singers like Billy Stewart, The Ink Spots, The Drifters and Doris Troy. It was as a member of Bluesology that Reg made his recording debut, playing piano on 'Come Back Baby' which was released as a single by Fontana in July 1965, just a few months after he left school. 'Words and Music by Reg Dwight' the sheet music proudly noted. More Bluesology records followed, including a second single also written by Reg. Elton John would never forget those first two singles: 'They were bloody awful, both of them.'

However, a lifetime later, Elton still retained some fond memories of his years with Bluesology: 'We used to play the Marquee, second on the bill to The Spencer Davis Group, Manfred Mann, The Herd. I remember Jimi Hendrix saying hello, and I thought that was really nice of him because he didn't know me from Adam.' During 1967 Bluesology landed regular work backing Long John Baldry, who had begun as an R&B singer working the same circuit as The Rolling Stones. Baldry's commercial breakthrough came later that year with an immensely successful ballad 'Let The Heartaches Begin', but by then it was all becoming too much for Bluesology's pianist: 'As Baldry's style changed towards the soft ballady stuff we moved into cabaret, and it was really

Reg Dwight, shortly after signing his contract with Dick James Music in 1968. Reg was ever the puppet-master, controlling his own image with a wise name-change to Elton Hercules John

beginning to bring me down.'

Bluesology continued to limp along, but on their way back from yet another gig up North, Reg finally decided that it was time for a change. 'Reg Dwight was hopeless, it sounded like a librarian.' And so, lifting the Christian name of Bluesology's saxophonist Elton Dean and the surname from their frontman Baldry, Reg Dwight was reborn as Elton John. In 1971 when he formalised the name-change by deed-poll, he added the middle name 'Hercules', apparently (says his mother) as an homage to *Steptoe and Son*'s cart-horse. The following year he borrowed the horse's name again, this time to re-christen a bungalow he had bought in Surrey, where he and manager John Reid would live for the next four years.

The original Elton – Elton Dean who went on to join Soft Machine – remembers the Bluesology pianist who borrowed his name: 'He didn't make mistakes. He didn't inspire you particularly. He was just Reggie – or Bunter, I used to call him, 'cos he was a little portly and always used to wear striped blazers.' One of the reasons for Reg's growing unhappiness with Bluesology was that the group gave him no opportunity to sing. He was employed as the group's pianist and no one seemed remotely interested in the songs he claimed to be writing, or in hearing him sing them.

Uncertain of his sexuality, concerned about his weight, unhappy with the direction his career was taking… as 1967 drew on, Reg Dwight found that the newly-emerged Elton John still had much to worry about. It was supposed to be the Summer of Love, but neither Elton nor Reg was getting much of that. And then one day an advertisement appeared in *New Musical Express* announcing that Liberty Records were looking for 'Artistes/Composers/ Singers/Musicians.' **ej**

I'm Gonna Be A Teenage Idol

Liberty Records' Ray Williams remembered a 'charming, shy, overweight little fellow called Reg,' coming into his Mayfair office in response to the *NME* ad. But Reg himself was not at all confident that he had made a favourable impression: 'I met a guy called Ray Williams who said "We all want to hear you sing." The only things I knew how to sing were the things I used to sing in the pub, which were Jim Reeves' songs; they weren't really looking for Jim Reeves at that time, so they weren't jumping up and down with glee at this overweight bespectacled thing looking like a lump of porridge singing a Jim Reeves song!'

Despite the unprepossessing appearance, Ray Williams was quite impressed by the intense young man who sang for him. And in a stroke of unwitting genius, when Elton mentioned that he wrote his own songs but didn't write lyrics, Williams recalled a folio of crumpled lyrics sent in on spec by a Lincolnshire teenager. He suggested that perhaps Elton might feel inspired to set some of these words to his melodies. That was the

moment, one fateful afternoon in an office in Albemarle Street, London W1, when the most successful British songwriting partnership since The Beatles was born.

Unlike Reg Dwight's rather troubled upbringing in Pinner, Middlesex, Bernie Taupin had spent an idyllic childhood growing up in the flat Lincolnshire countryside. But Bernie too was a solitary child, who always seemed to have his nose stuck in a book. Inspired by those books, and by the American country and folk music he heard coming out of the radio, he

soon began writing his own poems and lyrics. It was a package of these derivative and faltering first words, painfully picked out on an old manual typewriter in the farmhouse kitchen at his home in Owmby-by-Spital, which had found its way onto Ray Williams' desk in London.

By his own admission, Elton John could never fashion lyrics for himself: 'It was painfully obvious that though I could write a good melody, I wasn't really a words man. I never had the confidence to write down my feelings.'

Bernie Taupin can also vouch for his partner's inability: 'Elton is not a lyric writer. He just doesn't do it. . . one of the first songs he wrote was "I go to the witches' house, I go there whenever I can. Me and Molly Dickinson in my delivery van."!'

It was a testament to the success of Ray Williams' long-distance match-making that Elton had already written about twenty melodies to complement Bernie's lyrics before the pair even met each other. That first meeting, in July 1967, took place over a coffee at the Lancaster Grill on Tottenham Court Road. Bernie handed over some more lyrics, and the two young men hit it off immediately.

'I remember he looked quite angelic,' Elton later recalled, 'I really adored him from the word go, he was like the brother I never had, and it was wonderful being part of a relationship. It was not sexual, it was not physical, but it was emotional... He was the first real friend I ever had.'

So close did they become that Bernie moved in to share Elton's bedroom at 111 Potter Street, his mother's home in Pinner. The remainder of 1967 and much of 1968 was taken up with Elton putting melodies to Bernie's lyrics, and then venturing down into central London to demo their material at the studios of music publisher Dick James. When he learned that Elton and Bernie were spending so much time in his studio, James demanded to hear the results. He was sufficiently impressed by what

he heard to sign the two as a songwriting partnership.

The late Dick James was known as 'the luckiest man in British pop' – and not without reason. He will always be remembered fondly by a whole generation who grew up in the 1950s, for his stirring rendition of the theme song to ITV's *Robin Hood* series; but James would later find even greater fame when he came to own not only the publishing rights of the Elton John/Bernie Taupin partnership, but also those of the Lennon and McCartney song catalogue.

Unfortunately the luck didn't last and the relationships soured – to such an extent that in 1985 Elton John and Bernie Taupin sued in an effort to regain the copyright of the 144 songs they had written in the six years they were under contract to Dick James Music. It was a protracted case, and one which did not reflect well on Elton as it dragged through the courts. Elton and Bernie did eventually win back their copyrights, but the issues were clouded by the evident animosity and by the sudden death of Dick James just weeks after the end of the trial. His son Stephen has always blamed the legal wranglings for his father's death, maintaining that 'if it hadn't been for the strain of the court case and the impugning of his reputation...he would never have had the attack and might still be alive today.'

Elton spoke fondly of his former mentor after his death: 'Before we went to court, I tried to

Elton enjoys one for the
yellow brick road

Behind the dark glasses, a man with
a reputation for wearing his heart on
his sleeve

have lunch with Dick, I tried to say let's settle this and he wouldn't. And I stood in that box and I didn't hate him at all. I didn't enjoy the experience very much and we got this very big financial settlement. It was a shame, because I did have a good relationship with Dick James and it spoiled it.'

Back in the early days, prior to his breakthrough with 'Your Song' in January 1971, Elton John had paid his dues in the engine room of rock 'n' roll. He and Bernie were determined to persevere with their own original material – drawing heavily on the influences of Bob Dylan, The Band and The Beatles, while Dick James was understandably keen to push the partnership in a more commercial direction. The result was that acts with such un-hip names as Plastic Penny, Ayesha and singing-actor Edward Woodward were among the first to cover John/Taupin songs; one of their early collaborations, 'I Can't Go On Living Without You', sung by Lulu, was even shortlisted for the 1969 Eurovision Song Contest.

To supplement his weekly £15 stipend from Dick James Music (poor old Bernie was on an even more meagre £10 a week), Elton would hire himself out to help demo other writers' material. One of the most legendary occasions was a two-day session he undertook in 1970, singing the songs of writers from the Warlock Music stable – such eminent singer/songwriters as Richard Thompson, Nick Drake and John Martyn. Linda Peters – who went on to sing alongside and marry Richard Thompson – has good reason to remember working with Elton John on the Warlock sessions: 'It was the first time I'd been into a recording studio. I was petrified. I had valium after valium, glass after glass of wine. Elton was fabulous, a complete pro. I was absolutely wasted. We did two sessions, over a couple of days, at Sound Techniques in Chelsea. I don't remember much about it, except that Elton had to hold me up to the microphone. I can't listen to it, I'm appalling, but Elton's good.

'I don't think he had been in the studio very much before that but he was already 'Elton' then. I called him Elton, although some of the studio people called him Reg. Arrogant fools that we were, we were very sniffy about him. God, you know, he sings 'kant' instead of 'can't'! He was just this pop singer. John Martyn was especially apoplectic about this, you know; he was an artist and he just could not believe that this person was butchering his songs. He should be so lucky. I see Elton these days and I tug the old forelock.'

Although delighted to be kept busy as a session pianist during the dog days of the late '60s – among the hits he is known to have played on are Tom Jones' 'Delilah' and The Scaffold's 'Gin Gan Goolie' – Elton admitted to *Mojo*'s Cliff Jones that at the time he didn't always appreciate the calibre of the records he was working on: 'I got a call to go to Air

Studios in London where The Hollies were recording 'He Ain't Heavy, He's My Brother', played piano for them and that was that. You don't think anything of it at the time, but when you hear it back on the radio, the place where all the music is really tested, it sounded great.

'My speciality then was backing vocals – I'm on Tom Jones' 'Daughter Of Darkness', 'Back Home' by the England World Cup Squad and even some of the Barron Knights' stuff ... 'An Olympic Record' they did at Abbey Road. In wanders McCartney, he was in Studio Two and thought he'd pop in and see what the peasants were up to. Me and Bernie Taupin just froze and made some mumbling noises and he said a few things, then sat down and started to play the piano, told us it was the latest thing the band had finished, and it was 'Hey Jude'. Blew my fucking head apart.'

In his continuing effort to make ends meet, Elton also appeared on hits compilation albums from budget labels like Marble Arch and Music For Pleasure – the kind which sold for 14/11d and challenged 'Can you tell the difference between these and the original sounds?' He felt he had quite a talent for these forgeries as he explained to Cliff Jones: 'I'm quite a good mimic, so I could adapt my voice to whatever act it was. Singing lead on 'Saved By The Bell' by Robin Gibb, I had to sing in this dreadful warble and I couldn't get it so I ended up actually warbling my throat. I do a pretty good Leon Russell impression too.'

Well, actually yes, most purchasers could tell the difference. But it is both fun and illuminating to hear the young Elton, sounding pre-stardom exactly like he does today, singing hits by Dave Dee, Dozy, Beaky, Mick & Tich ('Snake In The Grass'), White Plains ('My Baby Loves Lovin'), Norman Greenbaum ('Spirit In The Sky'), Christie ('Yellow River') and Cat Stevens ('Lady D'Arbanville'). In 1994, an imaginative British reissue label put together as many of the Elton covers from that period as they could cram onto one disc and released it under the title *Reg Dwight's Piano Goes Pop*. *The Times* wrote approvingly of the album: 'With uniform gusto, the intrepid and versatile vocalist attacked songs from every area of pop... A month after duplicating Creedence Clearwater's 'Up Around The Bend', Elton made his American debut... There would be no more counterfeits; he had finally established his own identity.'

Once they have achieved that elusive megastar status, most artists would rather die than have their faltering first steps re-released for public consumption. But one of Elton's most charming characteristics has always been a total lack of pretentiousness about his work. His only stipulation was that his share of the artists' royalties should be paid to the Elton John Aids Foundation. **ej**

Elton is a strong vocal impressionist.
But he's always best being himself

A Rolls Royce for the true rock 'n' roll lifestyle – Elton pursued all the obligatory glitzy attributes of the super-wealthy

The Greatest Discovery

Once the Elton John bandwagon got rolling during the 1970s, there was no stopping it. As a performer, Elton became synonymous with all the excesses of the decade: from his lurid and flamboyant costumes to his all-or-nothing approach to the rock 'n' roll lifestyle. But underlying all the razzamatazz was the very real success which greeted every Elton John record release – particularly in America where he became indisputably the decade's most durable superstar.

At least one Elton single has appeared in America's *Billboard* chart every year since 1970. Even without the enormous trademark hats and platform boots, he towered over the American music scene in the 1970s – eclipsing solo Beatles, The Rolling Stones and Bob Dylan in the decade's album charts.

Between 1972 and 1975, Elton enjoyed an unprecedented seven consecutive No.1 albums in the US and with the release of *Captain Fantastic And The Brown Dirt Cowboys* he became the first act ever to debut at No.1 on the American album chart.

The Americans lapped up Elton's exuberant stage persona, too. Fans knew that when they went to see an Elton John show, they were going to get their money's worth: not just all the songs they knew and loved, but outrageously over-the-top showmanship as well. During his crazy performances during the 1970s, Elton appeared on stage dressed variously as Ronald McDonald, Ali Baba and Mozart. There was, however, at least one person who remained unconvinced about the wisdom of such costumes. Bernie Taupin worried, quite understandably, that all the fancy-dress antics might undermine the seriousness of his lyrics. 'Seeing Elton deliver something like 'Your Song' or 'Border Song' with Mickey Mouse ears or a Donald Duck outfit has never been one of my favourite things in life,' he admitted. 'Elton knows that I never felt any of that was necessary, but then I could be totally wrong and had it not been for the theatrics and the costumes, the glasses and the boots and the feathers and the colours, it wouldn't have gained the attention it did.'

In the mix – from one keyboard to another, Elton and Queen's Freddie Mercury add the finishing touches (with John Reid behind, left)

The shift in emphasis, from sensitive and introspective singer of Bernie Taupin's songs to glitzy showbiz posturing, could be traced back to a new presence in Elton's life – one which would continue to influence his career for the next 27 years. By the time he met John Reid, Reg Dwight had already become Elton John and his partnership with Taupin was well-established – the talent of the two men was self-evident. But in the fickle world of pop, talent is not necessarily enough. John Reid's contribution was recognising that Elton needed

to be a larger-than-life figure; and he swiftly set about re-modelling the youngster into a millionaire megastar, the 'Liberace of rock!'

Reid was born in Paisley in Scotland, the youngest son of John and Elizabeth Reid. In 1959, when John junior was ten, the family emigrated to New Zealand, but they became homesick for Scotland and within two years had returned home. A bright and smart pupil, Reid did well at school, but his business instincts soon proved stronger than his interest in schoolwork and he took a job at a men's fashion shop while still at school. He was from the start a brilliant salesman. He left school at 16 and began training as a marine engineer, but it was not long before the lure of London and the music business drew him down south. Reid soon managed to get work as a record plugger and one of the first artists whose work he promoted was the then-unknown Neil Diamond. In the event, Reid's rise was as rapid as Diamond's, and by the age of twenty he was in sole charge of the London office of the legendary Tamla Motown record label.

It was in 1970 while working for Motown, that Reid met Elton John for the first time, although it was not until later that year when both men were working in America, that they got to know each other well. It seemed an unlikely friendship – the two were so different in every way. But the relationship bloomed and within a year Reid was helping to run Elton's career and the pair were sharing a flat in central London. Early in 1972 the couple moved together to Wentworth, buying a bungalow which came complete with its own swimming pool and mini football pitch. Despite these distractions, as soon as they had settled in the couple turned their attentions once again to business. Later that year Reid took out a bank loan and set up a company – John Reid Enterprises – specifically to manage Elton John.

John Reid proved to be an incredibly successful svengali. He was barely twenty-five when he first astonished the record industry – by negotiating a record-breaking $5 million deal with MCA Records and in the process establishing Elton John as the biggest British act in America during the 1970s. Then having

pushed his boy to the top of the pole, he proceeded to pull off the even more difficult trick of keeping him there. The fact that today, after three decades at the top, Elton still remains a popular and much-loved star, is due in no small measure to John Reid's inspired managerial tactics. In 1976 when Elton moved to Woodside, the mansion in Old Windsor where he still lives, Reid did not accompany him. However the split was amicable and the two men continued both as friends and business partners. Elton even set aside a suite at his new home for Reid's exclusive use when he visited.

As befitted his position as King of British Pop, Elton's luxurious new home overlooked Windsor Castle. Costing £400,000 in 1976, the estate boasted three lakes, a large swimming pool, a squash court and numerous cottages and outbuildings. Inside there was more luxury than most boys from Pinner could even imagine – besides the cinema, snooker room, library and music room, there was a bar and disco which, should he feel like entertaining, could accommodate up to a hundred people.

Elton has always enjoyed his wealth, splashing out on records (at one point he owned over 25,000 LPs), houses, clothes, spectacles (207 purchased in just one impulsive spree), works of art, and countless other items that have appealed to him at one time or another. His acquisitive nature finally got the

With Kiki Dee for Elton's first UK
number one hit – 'Don't Go Breaking
My Heart'

better of him to the extent that there just wasn't house room for everything he was buying. There was no wall space left inside, so that a recently acquired Rembrandt etching had to be hung in the garage. Other new purchases simply remained in their packing cases and were stored in the outbuildings.

Eventually Elton faced the inevitable, and in 1988 decided to clear out his life with a spectacular sale of artefacts at Sotheby's; although six years later he still owned 3000

pairs of spectacles – enough to justify an exhibition in Italy of his costumes and eyewear. However it was not only on himself that Elton spent with such abandon, he was renowned for his generosity to others. Tales abound of whole orchestras receiving presents and cardboard boxes full of gold Rolex watches waiting to be given as gifts.

Nowadays Elton also has homes in Atlanta, New York, Paris and the South of France, but despite his increasingly glamorous lifestyle, those who know him well claim that even today Elton John is still capable of being as starstruck as the most gauche teenager. Certainly back then, at the time when they were being hailed as the new future of rock 'n' roll, Elton and Bernie were frequently both rendered speechless as the latest in a long line of their idols queued up to shake hands. At first it was near contemporaries, singer/songwriters like David Ackles and Tim Buckley. Then, as his career arched further skywards, the stars also got bigger. Before long it was Bob Dylan and John Lennon.

A genuine passion for music was always at the heart of Elton's life. Even after the release of his second album in 1970, he could still be found working behind the counter at Soho's Musicland shop, so that he could get copies of the new American import albums as soon as they came in. It was an enthusiasm he would never lose, and in later years he reflected with some satisfaction: 'I played on a Lennon album, I played on a Dylan album, so I'm alright. I've done something with my life.'

As his life went stratospheric during the 70s, Elton was increasingly able to indulge his whims, and that included meeting more and more of his heroes and heroines. He had become friendly with film director Bryan Forbes and his wife Nanette Newman who lived nearby, and they in turn began to introduce Elton to Hollywood chums like Peter Sellers, Mae West, Elizabeth Taylor and Steve McQueen. Groucho Marx, Leon Russell, Quincy Jones and tennis champions Jimmy Connors and Billie Jean King were among those who queued up to meet the new kid on

the block, and Elton remembers coming off stage one night and literally bumping into Cary Grant. But however grand the company, and despite his own fame and wealth, there were still plenty of occasions when glittering superstar Elton John was replaced by the shy, gauche Reg Dwight.

It was surely Reg, rather than Elton, who in 1981 splashed out £14,000 at auction for Spike Milligan's original scripts for *The Goon Show*. A long-standing fan of radio's most subversive and influential series, Elton explained that he had 'boughted dem because I loved dem.' Some years later Elton was among the star guests brought together in April 1998 for the BBC's official 80th birthday tribute to Milligan.

Like a medieval monarch, at the peak of his success Elton John could command the presence of whomsoever he pleased: he took the opportunity to duet with many of those he had admired from afar while he was still plugging away with Bluesology. He sang with Cliff Richard, Little Richard, Gladys Knight, Dionne Warwick and Stevie Wonder; he sang with up-and-coming talents such as George Michael, Jennifer Rush, k.d. lang and Marcella Detroit; and he sang alongside old mates such as Eric Clapton and Rod Stewart.

While never missing an opportunity to pay homage to early idols – Lonnie Donegan, Bob Dylan, John Lennon – Elton could always be relied upon to contribute pumping piano or

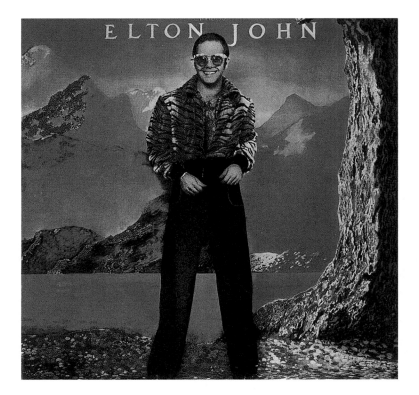

backing vocals to bolster the records of those whose nascent talent he admired – Jackson Browne, Kiki Dee, Lesley Duncan. He was equally generous in acknowledging his peers and at an awards ceremony in London during the late '70s, Elton graciously accepted the award for 'Best Songwriter', but admitted that he felt it should really have gone to Elvis Costello!

In spite of the numbing Saturday morning piano lessons and those endless Saturday night pub singalongs, Reg was always grateful for the God-given gifts which enabled him to escape from Pinner. And throughout his career, even during the worst of his personal problems, Elton has always taken the time to acknowledge his influences and encourage new talent. It is an endearing characteristic; and for someone of Elton John's stature, nigh-on unheard of.

Both Elton and Bernie remember those early years as the best of times. They were young and full of enthusiasm, buoyed up by being able to record their own music and optimistic for the future. The real breakthrough came in January 1971 with 'Your Song', and this was swiftly followed by a succession of unforgettable hits: 'Rocket Man'; 'Crocodile Rock'; 'Daniel'; 'Candle In The Wind'; 'Don't Let The Sun Go Down On Me'; 'Saturday Night's Alright For Fighting'; 'Goodbye Yellow Brick Road'; 'Someone Saved My Life Tonight'; and 'Sorry Seems To Be The Hardest Word'.

Try as he might though, Elton John could never quite reach the coveted No.1 spot. In 1976, 'Don't Go Breaking My Heart' – a duet with his old friend Kiki Dee – did finally take him to the top single slot. But he would be forced to wait another fourteen years before he could claim a solo No.1 single in his own country. ej

Elton's outrageous spectacles have commanded almost as much attention as his tunes – at one point he owned 3000 pairs

Dressed to excess – the flamboyant style of Elton John (with New York club owner Rodney Bingenheimer), taking 70s fashions by storm

Rocket Man

Throughout the 1970s, Elton John was a regular fixture on Radio 1's airwaves, despite an initially unenthusiastic response from the Beeb's audition panel, who in 1968 had rather harshly described the young singer's voice as 'thin, piercing... and with no emotional appeal,' whilst damning his songs as 'dreary, pretentious material'. Elton forgave them though, and one of his best-received sessions came in 1973 when, at the height of his fame, he guested on the Christmas Day edition of John Peel's show and ran through a repertoire cosily reminiscent of Reg Dwight's repertoire at Pinner's Northwood Hills Hotel – including 'Down At The Old Bull & Bush', 'Lily Of Laguna' and 'Knees Up Mother Brown'.

The worldwide audience for Elton's music continued to expand as the '70s drew to a close, and in 1979 he became one of the first rock stars to play in Russia. But all was not well within the Elton camp. His record sales were decreasing in both Britain and America and his health was beginning to suffer. On at least two occasions Elton was rushed to hospital with

Elton in one of his calmer outfits – the flamboyance this time strictly in his piano-playing at a concert in 1979

suspected heart attacks, although they turned out to be just stress-related false alarms. Up until this point Elton had been fond of boasting that he had 'the constitution of an ox. I would stay up all night for five or six days in a row and then go and do a rehearsal for a tour.' Now, however, the strain of year after year of over-indulgence was finally beginning to tell.

Even the long-standing writing partnership with Bernie Taupin seemed to have stalled in the wake of the perceived failure of 1976's *Blue Moves* album. Elton had always been the flamboyant other half of Bernie, he got up and did what Bernie only ever wrote about, but it was hardly surprising that Elton's penchant for the grand gesture could occasionally grate with his lyricist: 'Sometimes I thought it was detrimental to the content of the song if you're singing about attempted suicide while jumping up and down on the piano with 3ft boots on and mauve feathers sticking out of your head.'

The two men's names had been inextricably linked since they had begun writing together as teenagers – indeed when a collection of Bernie's lyrics was published in the '70s, the book was self-deprecatingly titled *The One Who Writes The Words For Elton John*. But while Elton was unquestionably the focal point during the glory years, it was Bernie who kept him supplied him with words to sing. As a lyricist, Bernie may not be as adept as boyhood idols like Bob Dylan, and he may have had a march stolen on him by the likes of Springsteen

and Elvis Costello, but over the years he has undeniably penned some of rock 'n' roll's most memorable couplets.

Bernie had already tried his hand at a patchy solo album in 1971, and by the time the pair split in 1976 he had relocated to Los Angeles, where he collaborated with Alice Cooper, Jefferson Starship and Heart. But although Elton's was the name in the headlines, Bernie too had his share of personal problems, including a divorce from his wife Maxine and battles with drink and drugs. His addiction led to the now familiar financial crises, and as the '70s came to a close, a chastened Bernie realised that those of his millions that weren't lost at the bottom of a bottle had already disappeared up his nose.

Typically though, he still had the honesty to appreciate what a pathetic figure he cut: 'I hate that press cliché of calling you a survivor just because you've got through binges of drink and drugs... There's nothing heroic in being a fall-down drunk... I hadn't cared about anything but getting wasted and having a good time. And suddenly came the day I realised it wasn't a bottomless coffer. The reserves were running dry.' A second marriage to American Toni Russo (sister of model-turned-actress Rene) in 1979 was Bernie's salvation, and soon after he began sporadically to write again with Elton. By 1983, the two were back working together regularly.

Even after the break-up of his second

marriage in the late '80s, Bernie remained in Los Angeles. He published a memoir of his Lincolnshire childhood, and in 1996 formed his own band, the promising country rockers, Farm Dogs. Now financially secure, his addictions conquered, and accepted as an American citizen, the flat Lincolnshire farmlands of Taupin's youth are far more than an ocean away. The boulevards and highways of Los Angeles are his home now. But in idle moments, Bernie Taupin must occasionally wonder just what road he might have travelled had his path never crossed that of Reg Dwight.

As Elton John dipped out of favour, memories of past glories and a massive personal fortune were no longer enough to bring him much comfort. His personal life was profoundly unhappy – and now his music too was suffering. Eventually even his loyal audience began to desert him and between 1978 and 1983 he did not enjoy a single top ten album in the UK.

More worrying still was the fact that Elton's addictive personality seemed increasingly to be taking control of his life. Beechy Colclough, a therapist who helped Elton work through his problems, said of him: 'He's a totally obsessive, compulsive person. He was born an addict. If it hadn't been the alcohol, it would have been the drugs. If it hadn't been the drugs, it would have been the food. If it hadn't been the food, it would have been the relationships. If it hadn't been the relationships, it would have been

the shopping. And, you know what? I think he's got all five.'

Despite a fading career Elton was still prime paparazzi fodder and he regularly appeared on chat shows and the covers of major magazines, but there was no longer any denying the dwindling records sales. Elton John was simply not the global superstar he had once been and it was with some trepidation that he entered the fallow years of the 1980s – a decade which for Elton John would prove as hollow as the 1970s had been successful.

If you were to pick just one high watermark from Elton John's stunningly successful career during the 1970s, it would probably be 7 May 1976, when he became the first celebrity from 'the world of popular music' since The Beatles to have a waxwork exhibited at Madame Tussaud's. But from that exalted position, there was apparently only one place left to go...

Even the wilderness years were widely publicised – Elton has always been happy to open his heart, and when he hit the skids, he hit them in typically frank and flamboyant fashion. Today, looking back, Elton can remember a time early on when he was happy, when the music was enough: 'The first five years of my career, I just loved every minute of it, I was making two albums a year, touring, I was totally involved. I was having a ball.' But it wasn't long before the glory years of the early 1970s were just dim and distant

*Bernie Taupin – 'the one who writes
the words for Elton John'*

memories and for most of the 1980s he existed in a blur of cocaine, sleazy stories and pointless extravagance.

Once Reginald Kenneth Dwight had been reborn by deed-poll as Elton Hercules John, he was destined to spend his life in the spotlight of unremitting media attention. Rock 'n' roll fame when it hits, hits big and by the mid-'70s Elton John was accounting for an astonishing 2% of all the records sold in the world. But by this time the man who made the music was no longer loving every minute of it and had already started searching for a means of escape. The causes of his unhappiness were many and diverse: his lack of hair; a constant battle with his weight; the painful legacy of a broken childhood home; unresolved confusion over the precise nature of his sexuality... all fuelled the bonfire of despair which had begun to rage.

The first suicide attempt had come even before the fame, while Elton was unhappily engaged to a girl called Linda Woodrow. The 21-year-old, unable to find a way to extricate himself from the relationship, put his head in the oven and turned on the gas. First though, he had taken the time to find a comfy pillow to rest his head on and had opened the window.

A more public attempt occurred in America in 1975 while he was at the very peak of his superstar fame. That week should have been among the highlights of Elton John's life: he would perform in front of 100,000 fans at two shows in the enormous Dodgers Stadium; the mayor of Los Angeles had designated it 'Elton John Week'; and they had even found space on the crowded Hollywood Boulevard for a star bearing his name. But Elton chose this moment to swallow sixty Valium and leap into a swimming pool in full view of his entire family who had flown over to help celebrate his success. Later he would remember that as they pulled him out, he could hear his beloved 75-year-old nan Ivy saying sadly, 'I suppose we've all got to go home now'.

Elton was tormented and confused and the unprecedented success he was enjoying on both sides of the Atlantic did not seem to be helping. Looking back on those crazy days, Elton admits that 'In fact my life wasn't a success. My career was a success. But my life was pretty miserable.' The following year his unhappiness was laid out in the open for all to see when he confessed to the American magazine *Rolling Stone* that he was bisexual. Four years before, David Bowie had become the first pop star to 'out' himself: 'I'm gay,' Bowie admitted to *Melody Maker*'s Michael Watts, 'and always have been, even when I was David Jones.' But Bowie was notorious for flirting with the media and was more than capable of playing out his androgynous charms to his own advantage. In another interview, this time with *Playboy* magazine, Bowie taunted the rival who was by then eclipsing his own career, calling Elton 'the Liberace, the token queen of rock'.

Under the headline 'Elton's Frank Talk: The Lonely Life Of A Superstar', the 7 November 1976 issue of *Rolling Stone* had Elton speaking openly for the first time about his sexuality: 'I don't know what I want to be exactly,' Elton admitted, 'I'm just going through a stage where any sign of affection would be welcome on a sexual level. I'd rather fall in love with a woman eventually, because I think a woman probably

lasts much longer than a man... I haven't met anyone I would like to settle down with, of either sex... There's nothing wrong with going to bed with someone of your own sex. I think everyone's bisexual to a certain degree. I don't think it's just me.'

Elton's first gay relationship had been with John Reid, the man who for many years – even after their relationship ended – managed his career. From the start Reid got on surprisingly well with Elton's mother; indeed it was Sheila who first suggested the idea that he should become her son's manager. It was a stroke of genius. Reid soon steered Elton's career to unparalleled heights. But the *Rolling Stone* interview made no mention of the relationship with Reid, although Elton had shared his life with him for five years, until just a few months earlier. He was however asked whether he and Bernie Taupin, with whom he had shared a flat right at the beginning of his career, had ever been lovers. Elton denied it emphatically and convincingly: 'No, absolutely not. Everybody thinks we were, but if we had been, I don't think we would have lasted so long.' **ej**

L-R: Beach Boy Mike Love, Who drummer Keith Moon and Elton attempt the famous Shadow step

The Bitch Is Back

Most of the passions in Elton's life seem in the end to have done little but contribute to his unhappiness. However, one love which has brought him huge enjoyment is the association with his beloved Watford Football Club. In 1974 Elton became a director of the club and two years later he was elected Chairman. He had the pleasure of watching from the directors' box as the club made a steady progress from bottom of the fourth division, until in 1982, they finally reached the first.

In 1984, Elton had the ultimate football thrill of watching Watford compete in the FA Cup Final against Everton, though sadly they lost, 2-0. Two years later on *Desert Island Discs,* Elton picked 'Abide With Me' as one of his pieces of music, specifically to remind him of Watford's great moment. He told Michael Parkinson that apart from getting married, 'that was the happiest day of my life'. In 1997, Elton chose the song again, this time performing it as his contribution to *Carnival,* a charity record in aid of the rainforests – 'this song always gives me goosebumps,' he explained.

When he took the bold step of admitting his bisexuality to the press, it was typical of Elton that his main concern was how the Watford fans would handle this issue: 'It's going to be terrible with my football club, it's so hetero it's unbelievable.' Mostly though, the revelation didn't diminish Elton's audience – except for a brief set-back in America's strict Bible Belt. The lurid new chants of away supporters included 'He's bald! He's queer! He takes it up the rear!' and 'Don't sit down when Elton is around' sung to the tune of 'My Old Man Said Follow The

Van'; but Elton coped with good grace and drew an important distinction between this spontaneous ribaldry and the kind of orchestrated attacks he had received from the *Sun* over the years: 'I took abuse – but it was good-natured, it was that English thing with a sense of humour. But I never felt afraid at football and I never felt threatened. The abuse I got at football is completely different to the kind I got from the tabloids.'

In Britain the 'Elton Is Gay' story was picked up by several newspapers, but they made little

*Elton John with his wife Renate Blauel
– before he came to terms with his
drug addiction and homosexuality*

of it and it didn't even make the front pages. His mother was upset at first, but swiftly came to terms with the revelations, saying: 'I think it was a brave thing for him to do. I would still like to think he could find happiness – with a male or female – I don't care.' In later years, Elton confessed that bisexuality was not the whole truth, in his words 'a cop out.' It had taken him a long time to admit it even to himself, but he knew now that he had always been homosexual. 'I was about 23 when I had my first gay experience. I probably realised before then that I was gay, but 23 was when it actually first happened. I dated women at school, I'd never gone out with a man. I was so innocent as far as sex goes. I went out with girls because

I didn't know what else I should do.'

Coming out as a bisexual had not created as big a media sensation as might have been expected, but neither had it done much to clarify things in Elton's mind. Evidence that Elton was still in some confusion about his sexuality came eight years later on Valentine's Day 1984, when he married recording studio engineer Renate Blauel in Australia. This time there was a sensation. The traditional white wedding, in St Mark's church in the Sydney suburb of Darling Point, made front pages all around the world. The pictures showed the bride in modest, full-length, high-necked, white silk and the groom resplendent in white tail-coat and straw boater. Both smiled shyly.

Despite his genuine candour and all the flamboyant camping it up, Elton had so far failed conspicuously to find any lasting personal happiness with anyone – of either sex. He had grown up in 1950s suburban London, watched his cousins marry and start families and unlikely as it may seem, as he approached 40, Elton John was still conservative enough to want to get married and father children himself. Both partners spoke with innocent optimism of the future they had planned together. Renate dismissed the tales she had heard about her new husband, saying simply, 'He's wonderful, the nicest guy I've ever met.' While he in turn offered a very clear picture of the kind of marriage they had in mind: 'We're not going to be the type of couple who go out to dinner parties and discos – I'm tired of them anyway. We just want to spend some time together. We want to have a home life. I simply want to be a family man – and I'm not getting any younger.' He had spoken about wanting to have children when he admitted being bisexual, perhaps now at last the time had come: 'I was an only child and I didn't enjoy that much. Ideally I'd like to have two, but you never know.'

It seemed such a simple dream, but inevitably the reality was not quite so straightforward. It didn't go unobserved when the couple's second wedding anniversary was spent apart, with Elton spending the day taking part in a French TV show *The Truth Game*, which featured famous people confessing all

to viewers who phoned in with questions. By the time of Elton's fortieth birthday the marriage seemed to be over in all but name. The huge party thrown for him by John Reid boasted 350 guests including the Duke and Duchess of York, five marquees, copious amounts of caviar and vintage champagne – but no Renate. Her absence was excused by illness, but the next day a statement was issued confirming that while there were no plans for divorce and they remained good friends, the couple had decided for the time being to live apart.

The marriage had lasted little more than three years, but for once the cliché of remaining on good terms seemed to be true. There was no evidence of resentment on either side and even in the immediate aftermath Elton had only good things to say about his ex-wife: 'I gave it my best shot and it's certainly not Renate's fault. She's done nothing wrong. That's what makes it so hard. I feel this terrible guilt because she was supportive when things were going badly for me. She was absolutely wonderful.'

A decade after the marriage ended Elton was still calling Renate, 'one of the classiest human beings on earth', but he seemed to have gained a little more perspective on what had gone wrong, confessing that he had hoped marriage, 'would save me from all the misery I was going through. I thought, "I'm gay, I'm very unhappy, I've been through all these relationships". But the basic truth of the matter was that I didn't address the real problem in my life which was I was a huge drug addict. That's the thing with drug addicts and alcoholics, they'll do anything but address the truth.'

Far from helping, fame had simply made it easier for him to feed his various addictions. Looking back, in 1995 he explained: 'I think there's a certain fascination: Let's go back to Elton's, there's bound to be drugs. I don't think I've ever used my celebrity status as such, but people are fascinated and they want to come back. So your celebrity helps out, it doesn't detract, it's definitely a plus sign.' Attempts at openness about his sexuality had not brought happiness, and neither had the ill-fated marriage to Renate. Now feelings of failure, isolation and bitterness, increasingly drove Elton to seek refuge in drugs, until eventually he was in the grip of a vicious addiction to cocaine, fuelled by his own unhappiness at who he was and what he had become.

Even at the time, Elton was disgusted with himself and with the drug abuse, but it was only in retrospect that he could see just how far he had sunk. He had also begun to understand that his addiction to cocaine was, at least in part, a result of the sexual unease which had haunted him since his days as a young boy in Pinner: 'I used cocaine basically for sex. My sexual fantasies were all played out while I was on cocaine. It made me insatiable for sex. Sometimes when I'm flying over the alps, I think that's like all the cocaine I've sniffed! As my mate Sting said, cocaine is God's way of telling you that you've got too much money.'

As well as drug binges, he was capable of being in his own words a 'vicious, nasty' drunk, 'mostly on vodka martinis, reducing all my best friends to tears – and the next day I wouldn't be able to remember.'

Besides music, Elton's other real passion has always been football and it was while he was Chairman of Watford FC during those dark years of over-indulgence, that Elton John was shamed by Graham Taylor: 'He was one of the few people who wasn't afraid of confronting me with my alcoholic problems. I went to a Boxing Day match in 1979, against Luton I think. I'd been up all night and went there, had a shave and he took me into his office. "I want to see you Elton," he says. So I go in and he's holding a bottle of brandy and he's going, "Here you are, fucking drink this, it's what you want isn't it? For fuck's sake, what's wrong with you? Look at the state of you. Get yourself together". He frightened the fucking life out of me.'

At the height of his fame, Elton's extravagance became legendary. He spent a fortune on champagne, Johnny Walker Black Label and vodka martinis, though he considered himself 'more a full-blown drug addict than alcoholic'. But during those years he did everything to excess and as if his problems with drink and drugs weren't enough, Elton's life was further complicated by bulimia, an eating disorder from which his friend the

From piano-player to football-player.
Elton's passion for football led to the
chairmanship of Watford FC. Even in
the strip, the wacky glasses stay

Princess of Wales also suffered: 'I would not eat for three or four days because I'd been doing coke and then I'd sleep for two days, then I'd get up and be starving hungry. So I'd have three or four pots of cockles, then I'd have three bacon sandwiches and then a pint of Haagen Dazs vanilla ice cream. So then I'd go and throw up, then I'd do the whole lot again. I'd throw up and it would be all down my dressing gown, there was no shame in anything I did.'

Eventually it got to the point where even Elton's most loyal supporter, his mother Sheila, couldn't face being around her only son. In 1987 she quit the UK to live in Minorca so that she would no longer have to watch the damage Elton was doing to himself. Sheila had watched

Elton's ears for music. Bernie Taupin always feared that the funny outfits would result in his lyrics not being taken seriously

her son grow from being a shy, talented pianist into an assured singer-songwriter and more recently into a global star – one of the most visible and recognisable people on the planet. But she was also keenly aware of the dark side of this success, and as a mother was terrified by the downward spiral in which Elton appeared to be trapped.

At the beginning, just being Elton John was enough for Reg Dwight. He had not only managed to make a career out of his music, but a very successful career. He hadn't had to compromise, and as the fame grew he enjoyed it more and more. But by his late 20s, with the world quite literally at his feet, he had succumbed to total rock 'n' roll madness. In Bernie Taupin's words Elton was now, 'Santa Claus one minute, the Devil incarnate the next.' Elton himself attributes many of his later problems, including the serious drug abuse, to childhood insecurities – and to the shy, chubby little Reg, who even the brash superstar Elton Hercules John could never quite banish.

Looking back Elton now sees quite clearly where his problems started: 'The first few years of your life are very formative and I was always very shy, very introspective, very insecure, overweight. I grew up in the 50s when kids were seen and not heard and I was always a bit of a goody-goody, too scared to join gangs.

So I rebelled against that in my late 20s and 30s, not in my teenage years. I missed the boat by about 15 years. So, you know, you take drugs, but you're still left with the same person. All those demons and all those insecurities were only heightened by the drugs when you came down from them. I didn't do any work on myself until I went into rehab and suddenly I'm left with this person that I've always been – little shy Reg from Pinner.' Of course, at the time things were not nearly so clear.

If ever there was an 'annus horribilis', Elton's was 1987. The year had started with throat problems, then his mother decided to emigrate and in November it was finally announced that he and Renate were to be divorced. All this personal anguish came at the worst possible time, while Elton was locked into a prolonged and bitter legal feud with the *Sun* newspaper over outrageous allegations they had begun to print in February. The battle was to rumble on for the rest of the year and most of 1988, taking a huge toll on Elton's strength and spirits. But the lower he plunged in that most terrible of years, the more he came to realise that the only person who could save him was himself.

It was to be a truly Herculean task, but with a determination that surprised everybody – not least himself – Elton John began the long, slow haul back to life. **ej**

The '80s saw a protracted battle between Elton John and the Sun newspaper after it printed an allegation that the singer – well-used to public speculation about his private life – felt unable to ignore

Dont let the Sun go Down on me

For John Lennon's 40th birthday in October 1980, Elton had sent him a card inscribed: 'Imagine six apartments, it isn't hard to do/One is full of fur coats, the other's full of shoes.' Like the rest of the world, Elton was horrified by the senseless murder of his friend in December of that year. His working partnership with Bernie Taupin also seemed to be over, another victim of the relationship problems from which Elton has always suffered. After the extraordinary highs of the 1970s, the 1980s did not appear to be shaping up well for Elton John.

The separation from his long-time lyricist was inevitable – both men were keen on the trial separation which would last on and off for seven years. Taupin remembers the relief: 'There was a time in the mid-'70s when you couldn't sneeze without hearing Elton John's name. You can't imagine the pressure. There was nowhere else to go and I just felt people must be sick of reading about us.'

Another long-standing connection which was severed during the 1980s was that with his

erstwhile music publisher Dick James. In the beginning it had been the old, old story: a pair of fledgling rock 'n' rollers, who would go anywhere, see anyone, sign anything to get their music heard… But that enthusiasm, and in particular the signatures volunteered with such naïve abandon, would eventually lead to a court of law and lengthy, bitter, recriminations.

With the growing realisation that rock 'n' roll was not just an overnight sensation but a multi-billion pound industry that would last for as long as there was electricity to power amplifiers, all those early agreements were being freshly and painstakingly examined. Contracts eagerly signed by unwitting teenagers in the days before compact discs, videos, compilation albums, film soundtracks, box sets or greatest hits packages could in later years cost them untold millions.

Following the break-up of The Beatles during 1971, rock stars seemed to spend as much time in court as they did in the recording studios. Everyone, from Bruce Springsteen to Gilbert O'Sullivan, went up before the beak in an attempt to wrestle back their past. George Michael, the Jimi Hendrix Estate, the Rolling Stones…all battled in the law courts over careless contracts signed way, way back, when pop stars were still being slotted into variety shows as a novelty act. Years on, those self-same novelties were at the epicentre of multi-million dollar organisations, and they were determined to keep it that way.

For most of his professional career, Elton John recognised the enormous debt he and Bernie owed to Dick James. At a time when he was struggling, it was Dick James who took Elton under his wing. Even after his astonishing success in the early 1970s, Elton maintained an affection for the avuncular man who had believed in him from the beginning. That affectionate personal relationship carried on well into Elton's superstar era, and it wasn't only Dick James of whom Elton and Bernie were fond, his son Stephen – who had increasingly taken over the company since his father's first heart attack in 1973 – was also close to the two men. The cordial relationship with the James family had survived even when John Reid took over as Elton's manager, and acted more and more as a buffer in business dealings between his client and Dick James.

Throughout his turbulent career, the Great British Public has remained enormously fond of Elton John. But the decision to sue his old mentor showed him for the first time in a different and far less appealing light. When the case came to court in 1985, Elton was seen as spiteful and vindictive, claiming back huge sums of money that he patently didn't need. And although Elton won his case, in February 1986 the death of Dick James from a heart attack soon after its conclusion only hardened public opinion against him.

The case limped through the law courts in 1985 and dragged on into 1986. At the centre

Don't let the Sun go down on me

Elton with a young George Michael in 1987 – the two would later pair up to sing the duet 'Don't Let The Sun Go Down On Me'.

of the hideously complex case was the question of song copyright. The 144 songs which Elton and Bernie had written, including 'Your Song' and 'Candle In The Wind', formed the basis of Elton's stupendous fortune, and the foundation for his career. Dick James had been down this road before, when in 1969 he had sold Lennon and McCartney's Northern Songs, earning the composers' lifelong enmity. Paul McCartney was equally distraught when The Beatles' back catalogue changed hands again in the 1980s, this time going to Michael Jackson.

Leaving aside the harsh economics, writers really do love their songs like children – they are, after all, a potent combination of childhood memories and diary entries. Throughout late 1985, Elton, Bernie and Dick James were familiar figures at the law courts in The Strand in London, painstakingly raking over contracts signed in another lifetime. It was a salutary reminder of the young Reg, who back in those pre-fame days was just another wannabee Dylan, or perhaps – with Taupin's help – a second Lennon and McCartney. But

*Another silly hat – this time a Gay
Hussar number – for Elton John*

the tanned and confident figure in the witness box was superstar Elton John, and in the end the judge found in his favour – returning the copyrights to him and Taupin. However, when it came to awarding royalty repayments, the figure fell far short of the eight figure sum anticipated by John Reid. It was a pyrrhic victory only and, while Elton won, the case did him a lot of harm.

The whole episode seemed tawdry. Dick James was bitterly upset by the personal animosity, believing right up until the case came to court that if he and Elton could sit down and talk together, like in the old days, they could sort something out without recourse to John Reid or the High Court. Elton also was

clearly unhappy at the way things turned out and following James' death he agreed to pay his legal costs. But by then it really was too late.

Musically too, the early 1980s were bleak years for Elton. Whatever else had gone wrong in his life, the music had always flowed easily and been well-received.

But without Taupin, for the first time Elton was really struggling with his career – singles such as 'Little Jeannie' and 'Sartorial Eloquence' came nowhere near the triumphs of 'Your Song' a decade before, while several 80s singles – 'Johnny B. Goode', 'Dear God' and 'Just Like Belgium' – failed to chart at all.

As he sailed past his mid-30s, Elton did at least manage to revitalise himself with a couple of strong new albums, *Too Low For Zero* in 1983 and 1984's *Breaking Hearts*. After years of being mocked by the Punks, he was suddenly fashionable again with New Romantic acts like Duran Duran and Adam Ant. Elton also found himself admired by the brightest of the decade's new superstars – George Michael, who as a teenager in the 1970s had grown up with Elton albums like *Blue Moves* and *Goodbye Yellow Brick Road*.

There were other new friends in even higher places – Prince Andrew asked Elton to perform at his 21st birthday party and a royal friendship resulted. In July 1986 Elton and his wife Renate were among the more unlikely guests at Andrew's wedding to Sarah Ferguson and in 1989 the boy from Pinner even found himself unexpectedly dancing with Her Majesty the Queen at Buckingham Palace: 'When I arrived there was no one there but the dance band and Princess Diana. We danced the Charleston alone on the floor for 20 minutes, then Princess Anne came up to me and said "Would you like to dance?" As we're bobbing up and down the Queen comes along with an equerry and says "Do you mind if we join you?" Just at that moment, the music segues into Bill Haley's 'Rock Around The Clock'. So I'm dancing to 'Rock Around The Clock' with the Queen of England.'

Princess Diana was also a fan of Elton's music and they were seen joking with each other at a number of Prince's Trust rock concerts during the decade. But it was Diana's increasing commitment to AIDS charities that drew them closer. At a time when AIDS hysteria was still rampant, Elton was moved by Diana's concern for victims of the virus. No one was more surprised than Elton himself at his patronage by the royal family, but by the middle of the 80s, particularly after his marriage on Valentine's Day 1984, Elton John seemed to have settled down to become a cosy part of the establishment. He could still do the crazy rock star bit when required – dolling

himself up like Mozart, or dressing up as Tina Turner to surprise the real Tina onstage – but the stunts no longer seemed so reckless. However, it was only a matter of time before the inner turmoil spilled over once again into the public arena, when Elton took on the might of Britain's gutter press.

Elton was no stranger to legal actions having spent much of 1985 in court struggling to free himself from the ties that bound him to his old boss Dick James. But his libel battle against the *Sun* eclipsed everything that had gone before, even though it was eventually settled out of court. Sordid allegations about Elton's penchant for bondage sessions with rent boys ran all over the *Sun* during February 1987, in the weeks leading up to his lavish 40th birthday party.

The *Sun* was the bête noire of English journalism during the 1980s. Editor Kelvin MacKenzie was a vociferous supporter of Prime Minister Margaret Thatcher's policies and it was undeniable that his newspaper's support was a major factor in helping Thatcher land a record three election victories. Proprietor Rupert Murdoch's notoriously anti-union stance had also infuriated many; as had the fact that the *Sun* was the first national newspaper to regularly feature tastelessly titillating photographs of topless models.

As much as they disliked the unthinking reactionary politics, it was the hypocrisy of the *Sun*'s innate conservatism, running side-by-side with its prurient near-pornography, which most incensed the chattering classes. Not the *Sun*'s 13 million regular readers though. Every day, they pored over the saucy pictures, salacious gossip and showbiz scandals and relished the opportunity of reading about lives broken apart 'in the public interest'. Rottweiler tenacity and paparazzi intrusiveness were undeniably effective at getting the paper its scoops, but in spite of the growing circulation, MacKenzie's bullishness and Murdoch's pursuit of profit at any cost both contributed to a feeling that the *Sun* was heading for a fall.

For Elton, the first shadows appeared on 25 February 1987, when the newspaper ran a story under the headline 'Elton In Vice Boys Scandal'. From early on it became apparent that the *Sun* – which had based its story solely on the evidence of a paid informer – was out to get Elton. But for once it seemed that they had misjudged the mood of their readership. In 1989, in an exhaustive piece on the battle between Elton and the *Sun* in the *Independent Magazine*, John Sweeney wrote of the affection in which Elton was held, suggesting that among the reasons for such public goodwill was the fact that his records had provided 'the noise wallpaper at our first parties and teenage discos' and that 'Elton did not, as Jagger and Lennon did, become a tax exile and disappear off into megastardom...'

Despite a welter of advice from friends and advisors, who were all firmly of the opinion that a court battle could only make matters worse, Elton was determined to clear his name. Even Mick Jagger counselled him against suing the newspaper over the allegations. Once the dirt started being turned over, he reasoned, the digging wouldn't stop. But the *Sun*'s allegations had hurt Elton personally, and upset his sponsors. The chocolate company Cadbury's, which had enlisted Elton's help for a massive TV advertising campaign, dropped him like a rotten Creme egg as soon as the drug stories and allegations of gay orgies began to appear.

Taking on the might of Britain's tabloid press undoubtedly carried enormous risks, both for his career and his personal life, but Elton was adamant. These accusations were potentially ruinous and they had been made repeatedly almost as if challenging him to deny them. Above all it became a matter of principal, as Elton said at the time: 'They can say I'm a fat old sod, they can say I'm an untalented bastard, they can call me a poof, but they mustn't tell lies about me.' This time he had simply been pushed too far. So, ignoring the cautions of everyone around him, Elton took the brave and possibly foolhardy step of instigating a libel action against the newspaper.

As soon as he started suing, the *Sun* unleashed its rat pack, and Elton's solicitor began to get reports that the newspaper was asking questions about the singer's allegedly deviant habits as far afield as Melbourne, Los Angeles and Scotland. The paper claimed to have procured compromising photographs of Elton – for which it paid £100,000 – but then came over all puritanical: 'The Polaroid photograph is simply too disgusting to print in a family newspaper' the editorial crowed. The fact was that the photos had nothing at all to do with under-age rent boys. But more importantly to Murdoch and MacKenzie, the Elton drama was beginning to hit the paper where it really hurt: in the circulation. Internal figures apparently showed that the newspaper was dropping sizeable numbers of readers (estimated at 200,000 a day) every time they ran an Elton/Rent Boy story.

Sun boss Rupert Murdoch was usually happy to let editor Kelvin MacKenzie go his own way with 'Britain's favourite newspaper', but when Elton announced he was suing, even Murdoch became worried. Concerned that the star might begin to boycott some of his world-wide television outlets, he rang MacKenzie early one morning and asked anxiously, 'Are we all right on this Elton John business?'

Murdoch was quite right to be worried, for there was a fatal flaw right at the heart of the Sun's scurrilous tales of sex and drugs romps. The problem was the date. The paper's main source, a rent boy dubbed 'Graham X', claimed that on 30 April 1986 he had taken two young boys to meet Elton for a gay sex session. But unfortunately for the Sun Elton was in New York on that day and he was able to prove that it wasn't until May 1 that he returned

to the UK on Concorde. There was no way that even Elton John could have been on two continents simultaneously.

Elton had found an ally in the Daily Mirror, which reported him saying: 'No matter what happens I will go into court, swear on the Bible and tell the truth about everything. I'm going to nail the paper that wrote all those lies.' The Daily Star was less sympathetic and when it chose to reprint some of the Sun's stories it too found itself on the receiving end of a writ. But by now the constant strain was beginning to show on Elton, who appeared on television spunky, but clearly dispirited. The unremitting media hysteria was further fuelled when the News Of The World entered the fray, claiming that its sister paper's allegations had denied Elton a knighthood in the Queen's Birthday Honours List.

The appearance of the Duke and Duchess of York at Elton's 40th birthday party in March gave a temporary boost to his morale and he was touched by the loyal support he received from the many fans who had applauded his decision to battle the homophobic tabloid. But the Sun persisted in its persecution and later in the year, apparently no longer content with 'kinky sex' stories, decided to have another go at Elton – this time over his pets.

On 28 September 1987, a story ran suggesting that 'vicious Rottweiler dogs' at Elton's Windsor mansion had been 'silenced by a horrific operation'. The piece went on to explain that Elton had authorised removal of the dogs' vocal cords so that he wouldn't be disturbed by their barking. Apparently no-one at the *Sun*'s Wapping HQ had paused to wonder what use guard dogs without barks would be, or for that matter to check their facts. The dogs, with vocal cords intact, were actually Alsatians and Elton sued the *Sun* for the 17th time. This last writ would be the first to come to court and Elton's lawyers intended to prove not only their client's innocence, but that he had never even owned dogs of that breed.

By November even their own sources had begun to desert the sinking *Sun*. Under the headline 'My Sex Lies Over Elton' the *Daily Mirror* ran an interview with the rent boy who had first made the accusations in which he admitted: 'I made it all up. I only did it for the money. I've never even met Elton John.' Realising at last that the game was up and they couldn't possibly win, the *Sun* decided not to risk being laughed out of court. However the apology was another 13 months in coming; and it was not until 12 December 1988 – the day set for the first court hearing – that the paper's front page boomed 'SORRY ELTON' and announced that it had agreed to pay 'megastar Elton John £1 million libel damages'.

Manoeuvring the preposterous 'Elton's Silent Dogs' story into court before any of the sexual allegations were even heard was a brilliant tactic by Elton's lawyers. The result was that things finally began to swing their way and

Elton was saved from the embarrassment of going into the witness box to endure a brutal cross-examination regarding the details of his sex life. The *Sun* crumbled. And it was the dogs what done it.

After nearly two traumatic years, Elton had won a £1 million settlement, a front-page apology and – perhaps most satisfying of all – watched delightedly as the *Sun* lost readers. What eventually brought the paper to its knees was the assertion that Elton John had mutilated his dogs, recalling Sherlock Holmes' observation on 'the curious incident of the dog in the night-time – "The dog did nothing in the night-time. That was the curious incident."'

At times Elton must have reflected ruefully on the irony of Bernie Taupin's line from 'Your Song': *'The sun's been quite kind while I wrote this song'*. For although in the end he had won the battle, the months of fighting had taken a heavy toll: 'I'm proud of the way I fought the *Sun*. It was a year and a half of sheer misery, but I was prepared to spend every penny I had. There were some days when I would get up and look at the front page of the *Sun* and just cry my eyes out. It was a constant battle.' **ej**

Musical matador Elton took on the Sun and won. He said that he had been prepared to spend every penny he had to make the newspaper retract its lies

For once Elton is out-glammed
– by Elizabeth Taylor

Reg Strikes Back

The world had long been perplexed by Elton's relationship with his wife Renate – by all accounts the marriage had effectively only lasted nine months, but the couple seemed determined not to give up on each other. More than ever during 1987 and 1988, Renate had proved herself to be Elton's staunchest supporter, helping him through both his battle with the *Sun* and a cancer scare which threatened to permanently affect his singing voice. Now however, just a few weeks before the date set for the first court hearing, it was announced formally that Elton and Renate were to divorce.

Looking back, Elton blamed the failure of his marriage on the various addictions which were crippling him at the time: 'When I got married I thought it would cure all that unhappiness in my life. Which is a complete addict's way of dealing with something, instead of addressing the problem – the fact that you take eight grammes of coke every night – let's move country, let's move house.'

As the 1980s drew to a close, with Renate

gone and all hopes of a 'normal family life' along with her, Elton looked increasingly bereft. He was hooked on drugs, addicted to alcohol and indulging in ever more frequent eating binges. Physically he was in a woeful state, but the psychological suffering was even worse. When he was sober enough to think at all, one particularly vivid image kept recurring in his mind: the shocking sight of Elvis Presley just before his death in 1977. The memory of that meeting had a chastening effect on Elton as he sat isolated in his mansion in Windsor, alone

with this haunting picture and the knowledge that his life, like Presley's, had become fogged by a miasma of drugs. 'He looked terrible,' Elton recalled years later, 'all bloated and hair dye trickling down his forehead. He had dozens of people round him, supposedly looking after him, but he already seemed like a corpse. I knew that if I didn't do something, I could end up in exactly the same way.'

Still awaiting the resolution of his battle with the *Sun* and knowing that his marriage was all but over, during 1988 Elton decided it was time

Costumes such as this came under the hammer in Elton's big Sotheby's clearout, which raised a staggering £15 million

to unburden himself of all (well at least some) of his worldly goods: 'You cannot stagger through life with all these possessions. This is kind of like watching your own death. Hopefully I'll still be alive when the sale comes up in September.'

The purging process began with a press release from Sotheby's announcing that Elton was to 'dispose of his entire collection of antiques and art'. The sale was a voyeur's paradise. Elton's profligacy had long been legendary, but the auction finally gave the world permission to be prurient. Just as in the last reel of Orson Welles' masterpiece *Citizen Kane*, the contents of Elton John's very own rock 'n' roll Xanadu were laid open for the world to see – including some that he'd never even got round to unpacking.

'It was like Harrods' warehouse,' Philip Norman quoted Elton as saying. 'There was stuff sitting unopened in crates, which was preposterous. Literally everything was covered, every wall, every surface. It was suffocating me.' Finding the will to begin ridding himself of that 'suffocation' was a real psychological breakthrough for Elton. It took a fleet of pantechnicons three days to move the numbered lots from his Windsor mansion to Sotheby's central London offices. As well as Elton's own memorabilia, there was an awesomely wide-ranging collection of art and artefacts. Paintings by Magritte, Warhol, Lowry and Picasso all fell under the hammer, as did Cartier watches and Tiffany lamps. Such was the intense interest in the four-day sale that the individual catalogues ('Stage Costume and Memorabilia', 'Jewellery', 'Art Nouveau and Art Deco' and 'Diverse Collections') were themselves boxed up and sold off by Sotheby's at £50 for a set.

Two thousand lots were listed, including all Elton's stage costumes, Judy Garland's camisole from *Meet Me In St Louis*, a souvenir programme signed by Elvis Presley, 150 Art Nouveau lamps... The auction eventually raised just under £15 million, with a million of that coming from items of personal memorabilia which Elton had hoarded throughout his near twenty year career. The most expensive Elton-related item in the sale was a pair of unfeasibly large skinhead boots he had worn in Ken Russell's 1975 film of *Tommy*, which were sold for £11,000 to a director of the company which makes Doc Marten boots. Also under the hammer were: 'Elton' illuminated novelty spectacles (£9,000); American Flag spectacles (£2,000); a signed photo of Elvis to Elton (£2,500); the Dodger Stadium suit (£6,200); and a *Captain Fantastic* gold disc (£5,600)... It was an astonishing cornucopia.

The contents of Elton's home had filled Sotheby's and the sale was an important symbolic cleansing of the 'old' Elton, but still it seemed as though his life lacked purpose. Even his victory over the *Sun* had in the long run done little to calm the demons which had once stalked Reg Dwight and now haunted Elton

Elton John does Wolfgang Mozart – another pretty good pianist – in concert in 1986

John. But in June 1990 some real career satisfaction came his way when, after nearly 20 years of hits, 'Sacrifice' at long last gave Elton his first solo No.1 in Britain.

Perhaps even more significant was the fact that he had pledged the royalties from this and all future singles to AIDS charities.

As a gay man, Elton was obviously acutely aware of the impact of AIDS, not only on the gay community, but on the world at large. In

1976 he had personally experienced a homophobic backlash when, following his admission of bisexuality, a number of American radio stations banned his records from their airwaves.

By the 1980s AIDS hysteria was raging and the deaths of celebrities such as actor Rock Hudson had already sent out shock waves. But for Elton it took the struggle of a sick schoolboy in Indiana to provide the focus which was so badly needed in his life. A whole world away from the glitter of Elton's jet-setting social whirl, a young man called Ryan White was slowly dying.

Ryan was a haemophiliac who had been infected with the HIV virus through a contaminated blood transfusion. Ryan was not himself gay, but such was the stigma and prejudice surrounding the disease, that he and his family were forced to abandon their home in order to escape the persecution of their neighbours. Elton was so moved when he read about the boy's bravery that he went out to Indianapolis to offer support to Ryan and his family. He stayed for a week and was there by Ryan's side when he died aged only 18. Elton stayed on to comfort the family and to help with organising the funeral and then, on 12 April 1990, he helped to carry Ryan's coffin. It was a moment he would never forget: 'It made me realise what an insane fantasy lifestyle I was living, seeing Ryan and his mother forgive all the people who had been so vile to them...

Seeing how brave that kid was I just knew then that my life was completely out of whack.'

Ryan's death brought Elton's life suddenly and sharply into focus: 'I just thought "Elton, your life is so fucked up, you're so out of proportion... This woman is losing her son, she's been living with him through this, she's always known he was going to die and now it's happening she's forgiving the people who were violent and nasty towards her in the first place and you haven't got the humility in your life, you complain about everything..." So that was when the penny dropped that my life was out of order, all my priorities in life were wrong and a relatively short time after that I went into rehab.'

The problem was that there were so many things wrong with his life that Elton was turned down by all the regular detox clinics for having too many addictions. Eventually though he checked into The Parkside Lutheran Hospital in Chicago and began working to get his life back on an even keel. The hospital treated all patients equally, expecting them to share the chores. Elton admitted that his main worry on the way to Chicago was that he wouldn't be able to operate the washing machine. One of his first tasks was to write a lengthy farewell letter to cocaine. The letter was so heartfelt that when Bernie Taupin read it later he admitted that he was moved to tears.

Elton was especially pleased that finally coming to terms with his addictions also brought about a reconciliation with his mother

Sheila who, unable to cope with her son's mounting problems, had spent the last three years abroad: 'She'd write to me. I'd cry when I read her letters. The funny thing is while she was in Minorca her health got bad. Since she got home, she's been perfectly well. It must have been all psychological, because of worrying about me.'

So determined was he to stay clean and sober, that in the first few years of his recovery Elton attended over a thousand meetings of Alcoholics Anonymous, Narcotics Anonymous and other recovery groups. Rumour had it that he only stopped when he began to fear that he was once again becoming addicted – this time to addiction therapy.

However, it seemed only natural that after 20 years as a celebrity, Elton should revel in the new-found anonymity of groups where people accepted him as a real person and understood his struggle to conquer his addictions. This was no longer the rather petulant superstar who would worry about the colour of his hotel rooms and aeroplanes, or complain that there was too much wind on the balcony.

In 1991 the death of Freddie Mercury from AIDS again motivated Elton and the proceeds from his duet with George Michael – a live version of 'Don't Let The Sun Go Down On Me', which was one of Elton's three favourite songs – all went to the Terence Higgins Trust AIDS charity. The song took Elton to No.1 again, though he initially had reservations about releasing it as a single: 'I didn't think it was going to be a hit. I said "George, this is a very crucial time for you. You've had this album out which hasn't been as successful as *Faith*, maybe you should think twice about putting a live single out." Of course, it was No.1 in every country in the world.'

At the Freddie Mercury Tribute concert at Wembley on 20 April 1993, Elton performed 'Bohemian Rhapsody' and, in a surprise move, duetted with controversial Guns 'n' Roses singer Axl Rose on another Queen song, 'The Show Must Go On'. It was a strange pairing, because over the years many of Rose's statements and lyrics had been perceived as anti-gay. Elton though was unfazed: 'I am not an exciting performer per se any more,' he admitted candidly. 'I was when I was younger, but those days of doing handstands on the piano are gone. Axl is exciting though. You need energy and he provided it.'

Elton John almost certainly donates more money to charity than any other British musician and in 1993 The Elton John AIDS Foundation was established to bring all the various charitable gifts under one umbrella. To date the foundation has raised over £9 million. The money is distributed in grants: 'It goes to direct care and education. I've got so many friends who need the money now for food, medicine. I'd rather give the money to people who need the support now.' ej

*Chalk and cheese, but Elton John and
Guns 'n' Roses' Axl Rose pulled together
to honour the memory of Freddie Mercury*

Elton used to hate being stuck behind the piano – he wanted to be a showman like Jimi Hendrix. The answer was to do handstands on it. Not your average pianist

Circle Of Life

Cutting free of the past was, as Elton had already proved, a vital part of the process of healing. In 1993 he took another symbolic step toward the future with the sale of 25,000 LPs at Bonhams. 'It was sad,' he admitted, 'they all had R.Dwight written on them and my little catalogue number, R.Dwight 001. Very sweet. I like things, but you can't become too attached to them.' Like many of his generation, Elton still regretted the passing of long-playing vinyl records and their replacement by the new and much smaller compact discs: 'There was

nothing like getting a gatefold album, Joni Mitchell or something, with a pair of headphones and the lyrics and disappearing into your own world... It's much harder with a fucking CD. You need a magnifying glass.'

Perhaps it was no coincidence that as Elton worked harder than ever to reclaim his life, so the quality of his music also improved. Post-rehab albums such as *The One* and *Made In England* have found him happily reunited with lyricist Bernie Taupin and once again producing a seamless series of pop hits.

However, he is only too well aware of how hard it can be to grow old gracefully in rock 'n' roll: 'I am part of the rock establishment. The thing is that I sit behind a piano. Years ago I hated it. I wanted to leap around and be a singer and I was stuck behind a piece of wood, that's why I used to jump up and down on it and stomp on it. I wanted to be Jimi Hendrix. Nowadays I'm glad I'm stuck behind a piano. I hope I'll be singing music for the rest of my life. I don't want to do anything else. The Queen Mum of Pop is definitely what I've been saddled with. If that's

what it is then it's fine with me. At least it's the Queen Mother – most respectable member of the Royal Family!'

The real Queen Mother is another of his royal friends and she is known to particularly admire the view of Windsor Castle as seen from the grounds of Elton's mansion. Bernie Taupin remembers sitting next to her during dinner at Elton's one night. She pointed out of the window to the flag on Windsor Castle and casually remarked 'that means my daughter's at home'. Princess Margaret too would sometimes pop over from Windsor for tea, often accompanied by her children. On one occasion Elton returned the patronage by commissioning her son Viscount Linley to make him an elaborate £75,000 bed.

In 1993, six years after his epic battle with the *Sun*, Elton took out another libel action – the first against his former ally the *Daily Mirror*. This time the problem centred around his bulimia: the paper claiming that the revelations about his eating disorders had been part of a publicity stunt. Once again Elton sued and won, coming away with another £350,000.

With his career apparently back on track, Elton was delighted to be asked by Walt Disney to come up with an original score for its latest full-length animated feature *The Lion King*. Paired with Tim Rice who had worked on Disney's *Aladdin*, Elton buckled down to the discipline of scoring music for a film and, in a mere 90 minutes, came up with the haunting opening theme, 'Circle Of Life'. On its release in 1994 *The Lion King* was, predictably, a huge draw at the box-office. But perhaps more surprisingly, the new songwriting partnership also proved to be a great success and in 1995 the pair were awarded the Oscar for Best Original Song for 'Can You Feel The Love Tonight' from *The Lion King*.

Following their triumph at the Oscars, Elton and Tim Rice helped to transfer the story from the screen onto the stage. They added three new songs to their original score and in

November 1997 were present at 42nd Street's New Amsterdam Theatre to witness their conquest of Broadway. The critics were enchanted by the show. The *Daily Mail* purred: 'The *Lion King* cartoon has been brilliantly and irresistibly made over for the stage. It looks set to be a fixture for years to come.' *USA Today* predicted that 'it may run as long as its tamer cousin *Cats*' while the *New York Post* could barely contain its enthusiasm: 'Unquestionably Disney's new jungle package is enormous, fantastic, riotous fun. The first word that springs, leaps, nay pounces, to mind is simply extraordinary,' it gushed.

Success on Broadway doesn't necessarily reflect record sales; sure-fire successes can flop and one-off unknowns have been known to run and run. In the months following *The Lion King*'s opening, Paul Simon's ambitious Broadway musical *The Capeman* opened and, shortly afterwards, closed. But advance ticket sales for *The Lion King* were a healthy £12 million and it looked as though Elton would soon be able to add Broadway to his other triumphs. Following their successful collaboration on *The Lion King*, Sir Elton and Sir Tim were soon working together on another project – said to be an adaptation of Verdi's *Aida* for a forthcoming Disney animated feature.

For Elton, 1995 turned out to be a vintage year. As well as collecting an Oscar, he was made a Commander of the British Empire and awarded the Polar Music Prize by the King of

*Bernie Taupin with Elton – together
again after a protracted break from
their writing partnership*

Elton's penchant for silly hats
developed in part because of his
concerns about his thinning hair – a
problem he has since remedied
through extensive transplant surgery

Sweden. He even had the honour of becoming the first rock star ever to be awarded Honorary Membership of the Royal Academy of Music. It seemed an altogether fitting reward for the chubby lad from Pinner who had made his way so dutifully to Marylebone Road for piano lessons during the grey days of the 1950s.

Diligent piano student and tiresome superstar. Addictive personality and effortlessly fluent musician. Outrageous showman onstage; shy, insecure and troubled offstage. A man capable of gross examples of superstar petulance, but equally capable of tremendous generosity. There have been times when he seemed little more than a mass of contradictions, but over the years Elton John has become firmly established as a unique and much-loved part of the British landscape.

Happily settled for some years in a monogamous relationship with Canadian film-maker David Furnish, Elton seems happier at the end of the '90s than ever before. His weight under control, his addictions a chastening memory, he is though, still capable on occasion of being the flouncy Elton of old, as the 1996 television documentary *Tantrums and Tiaras* displayed. The film, a warts-and-all depiction of superstar life directed by his long-suffering partner, included one hilarious scene which showed Elton vowing never to return to France after a fan had the temerity to wave at him while he was playing tennis. 'I take my tennis seriously,' he blustered, vaguely trying to justify

the outburst. Hard though to think of another star of his calibre who would allow such a candid film to be made and shown: 'I wanted to say "Listen, I'm not Cliff Richard. This is how unbearable I can be and, sometimes, how endearing I can be."'

The wave of tragedy which engulfed Britain in the autumn of 1997, in the wake of the death of Diana, Princess of Wales, lapped over well into the new year. Early in 1998, 'Candle In The Wind 1997' won a Grammy Award for Best Male Vocal Performance; and at the end of May, it scooped three awards at the prestigious Ivor Novello Awards, including a special award for the two composers. In his acceptance speech Elton confessed to mixed feelings: 'This is a bittersweet award to get. I wish the record never had to be made.' The song seemed to have taken on a new life all of its own and simply wouldn't go away. But for Elton, the time had come when the grieving had to stop.

Earl Spencer's plans to hold a concert in memory of his sister in the grounds of Althorp, the family's Northamptonshire home where Diana was buried, attracted much criticism – not least from Elton John who, thanks to that song, has become indelibly linked with the tragedy of the late Princess's death. It was hoped that other stars of his calibre, like Paul McCartney and George Michael, would appear at the £40-a-ticket Memorial Concert, but as the rumblings and grumblings continued, it was less fashionable names such as

Elton John with Tim Rice, lyricist for the film music Elton scored for the Disney hit The Lion King – which the pair later successfully developed for Broadway

Chris De Burgh and Cliff Richard who were coming forward.

'I think it's time to give it a rest,' announced the newly ennobled Sir Elton John on *GMTV* in March 1998. 'I'm not sure about the concert and I'm not sure of all the ideas about perpetuating the thing. I'd like to remember her in my own private way and I'm not going to be bouncing on stage and doing any concerts in memory of Princess Diana. I've done what I've done and I'd like to leave it alone.'

Meanwhile the awards and statistics carry on accumulating. He has now racked up total record sales of 150 million, making him –

second only to Paul McCartney – the UK's most successful musical export. And worldwide interest in Elton John continues to snowball. In October 1997, this was given a further boost when the world's publishers gathered at the Frankfurt Book Fair to sell their wares. The main talking point was Elton John's possible autobiography – the book trade was buzzing with the news that, finally, Elton had decided to tell all. However in the end, according to *The Bookseller*, 'the huge advance being demanded, rumoured to be between £8m and £10m, was regarded by many as "silly money". There was also doubt that the

*Elton John with partner David Furnish at a show for fashion
designer Gianni Versace – another close friend of Elton's
whom he was to lose in tragic circumstances*

singer could add much to the amount already known about him.'

In 1998 when Pet Shop Boy Neil Tennant put together the album *20th Century Blues* to pay tribute to the songwriting genius of Noel Coward and at the same time raise money for the Red Hot and Blue AIDS charity, Elton was there representing 'The Old Guard' – along with Paul McCartney, Bryan Ferry and Sting. Indeed it was he who closed the album – following performances by young turks like Suede, Space and The Divine Comedy – with a knowing rendition of the title track.

Mind you things weren't always so cosy in the vintage rock star club. Just to prove that pop feuds didn't always have to be between brothers from Manchester, towards the end of 1997 there was a well-publicised spat between Elton and the Rolling Stones' Keith Richards. When Keith opined that Elton's talent was 'limited to singing songs for dead blondes', Elton responded in kind: 'He's pathetic. It's like a monkey with arthritis trying to go onstage and look young. It must be awful to be like Keith.' Earlier in the year, when asked if they were appearing at the upcoming Princess Diana tribute concert, it had been Keith who famously declined on behalf of the Stones with the immortal words: 'I never met the chick.' **ej**

Liberace eat your heart out: as over-the-top as costumes can get, this Louis XIV number required serving boys to allow Elton to move at his 50th birthday bash

Made in England

As the 20th Century wound down, there was no getting away from Sir Elton John. The former Pinner man had been made a CBE by the Queen in 1995, but in February 1998 a knighthood 'for services to music and charity' was the crowning honour. Elton was not the first rock 'n' roll knight, having been pipped to the post by Sir Paul McCartney who was ennobled in 1997. Bob Geldof and Cliff Richard had also received knighthoods, but not for music – theirs were bestowed upon them specifically in recognition of their extensive charity work.

Clearly captivated – despite being announced by the Lord Chamberlain as 'Sir John Elton' – the new Knight Bachelor was accompanied to Buckingham Palace by David Furnish, his mum Sheila and step-father Fred. It was a moment of highly-charged emotion for Elton and indeed for his mother. She had been with him every step of the way, from the solitary, suburban childhood, through the high-rolling years of fame and wealth, the coming to terms with his sexuality, the turbulent decline of drink and drugs…and all culminating in

seeing her only son tapped lightly on both shoulders by Her Majesty the Queen.

'They don't come much bigger than this,' Elton John enthused to *Hello!* 'To be knighted by the Queen with my mum and dad here is fantastic. I am extremely proud. I love my country and to be recognised in such a way – I can't think of anything better... I've had a long career and worked hard, but I think the turning point came in 1990 when I got sober and started to do some charity work, particularly for the AIDS problem. A knighthood is

the icing on the cake.'

Despite the considerable contributions to charity, Elton remains equally well known for his prodigious appetite for shopping. Pinned to the door of the fridge at his Windsor home is a sign reading: 'Of course I need it today. If I wanted it tomorrow, I'd order it tomorrow!' Now that he has quit drugs and drinking, Elton cheerfully admits that shopping is his 'last remaining vice.'

In November 1997, Elton decided to sell off the past three years' worth of accumulated shopping. Rather than holding a scaled-down version of 1988's Sotheby's auction, Elton elected to sell directly to the public by opening his very own shop. Temporary premises were found in London's Piccadilly and stocked with 10,000 items which had cost Elton £2.5 million. The items were to be sold at 10% of their original value, and the £250,000 raised all went to the Elton John AIDS Foundation. Soon after this bout of retail therapy, the American bank Citibank, with a nice eye for irony, chose Elton as the public face of its high value current account – for households with an annual income in excess of £30,000.

Over the years, Elton has made no secret of his compulsion to spend, spend, spend: 'I could find a shop in the Sahara desert,' he once joked. But he was incensed when supposed details of his credit card transactions were leaked to a national newspaper early in 1998. The paper alleged that Sir Elton frittered £280,000 in a single week, and went on to chronicle the star's alleged purchases. Soon after the story broke, John Reid Enterprises announced that they would be taking legal action against the *Daily Mirror*, the hacker who had apparently gained access to the company's computer records and PR consultant Max Clifford who had put the hacker in touch with the *Mirror*.

At the time there was no sign of any friction between Elton and John Reid, the man who had steered his career so successfully and for so long. But it has since been suggested that it was these revelations concerning Elton's spending which led to their parting. Even music business insiders were stunned by the news that the pair were to split. 'It's like Colonel Parker quitting Elvis,' said one when the news broke in May 1998. When the couple ceased living together in the mid-seventies their business relationship had survived and from then on it seemed that the partnership would endure anything. It was after all Reid who helped transform the shy boy from Pinner into multi-millionaire superstar Sir Elton John.

For nearly thirty years Reid had played Svengali to Elton's Trilby, focusing all his considerable energies on the business side of Elton's life and thus allowing the singer to concentrate solely on his music – and shopping. 'We are equipped to take care not only of Elton's professional career,' Reid explained in 1990, 'but the business side as well – legal, accounting, tax planning and so on.' Reid's devotion to his client was legendary. Almost as legendary as his ferocious temper, which has seen furniture hurled around offices, critics physically threatened and staff sacked en masse. But it was Reid who had first taken the withdrawn and somewhat gauche Elton in hand and steered him towards the now familiar champagne and caviar lifestyle. And over the years since then he had continued to prove his loyalty, protecting Elton fiercely.

John Reid did not discover Elton, as is so

Elton (with David Furnish) becomes
Sir Elton, knighted by the Queen
for his services to music – the only
other popular musician to have
been similarly honoured for this
reason is Sir Paul McCartney

often suggested. Nor did he pair him with his songwriting partner Bernie Taupin; by the time Reid arrived on the scene, Elton was already making records. But since those very first hits over a quarter of a century ago, Elton's entire career had been brilliantly engineered, one might even say masterminded, by his friend and manager. The fact that in the notoriously transient world of rock 'n' roll, Elton John has remained at the top for nearly three decades is surely, at least in part, the result of Reid's skilful management. Just compare his rise and rise

with the careers of piano-playing pop contemporaries like Gilbert O'Sullivan or Lynsey De Paul – while they are all but forgotten, Elton's career appears to go from strength to strength.

Despite a spell managing Queen, Reid's main managerial commitment was always to Elton. In the past he had handled Billy Connolly, Pamela Stephenson, Dame Edna Everage and more recently *Riverdance* creator and star Michael Flatley – but in June 1997 that business relationship also ended tumultuously

*Elton re-opens The Landmark,
a drop-in centre for people
with HIV and AIDS, in 1994*

when Flatley dismissed Reid, who promptly sued the dancer. Reid's relationship with Elton was different though, it was never purely business. In the early years, Reid had been instrumental in encouraging Elton to keep the matter of his sexuality a secret, fearing for the effect on his career. When, in November 1976, Elton gave an interview to *Rolling Stone* magazine in which he finally admitted being bisexual, Reid bitterly regretted the star 'coming out' to the American magazine.

In 1984 at Elton's wedding to Renate, Reid shared the Best Man duties with Bernie Taupin. Six years before, he had himself become engaged to Sarah, the 18 year-old daughter of Bryan Forbes and Nanette Newman, although the engagement was called off just a few weeks later. By the time of Elton's 40th birthday in 1987, his marriage to Renate seemed over, but his friendship with John Reid was still strong. Reid hosted a lavish party for the birthday boy and bought him an £80,000 Ferrari Testarossa.

Just a few months before the surprise split, Reid was once again a guest, this time at the party to celebrate Elton's 50th birthday. He used the occasion to speak fondly and publicly about how the singer had helped him over his own battle with alcoholism. While outsiders may laugh that recently John Reid has had little to do but count Elton's money, the manager knew better: 'He has no interest in money for its own sake,' Reid grumbled in 1997. 'The world is a giant toy store. I'm forever hounding him to

save money. He'll say "What for?"' Nonetheless Reid has succeeded to the extent that Elton now shares the position of Britain's second richest rock star with his old rival from the early 70s, David Bowie.

The very public and bitter break-up has left the music business in shock. Managers are often shadowy, behind-the-scenes figures, but Reid has always been a highly visible member of an elite group of pop masterminds. The first and most famous of these was Colonel Tom Parker, who in the 1950s turned Elvis Presley into the biggest cultural phenomenon of the post-war era. In the '60s Brian Epstein lifted the Beatles out of Liverpool cellars and took them to the world, and in the '70s it was John Reid who transformed Elton John from a sensitive singer into an international superstar.

How the break-up will affect the careers of the two men remains to be seen. A new company, Elton John Management, has been set up and will be run by Colin Bell who resigned as Managing Director of London Records to take up this new challenge. Following the incredible success of 'Candle In The Wind 1997' and his knighthood, it seemed that nothing could topple Sir Elton John from public favour. John Reid's personal fortune is conservatively estimated at £28 million, so there is no real need for him ever to work again: Reid has come a mighty long way from his working-class Glasgow boyhood and his other business interests have at various times included owning a London restaurant and a part-share in the Edinburgh Playhouse. He was also for a time a co-director of Elton's beloved Watford Football Club. But for over a quarter of a century, both his personal and business lives have been inextricably linked with those of Elton John. Now those ties have been broken, the question for John Reid must be, 'Where do I go from here?'

A late and less well-known passion is Elton's fondness for flowers and gardening. Deciding that he liked what Sir Roy Strong, former Director of the Victoria and Albert Museum, had done with the late Gianni Versace's garden in Como, and with money (as usual) no object, Elton asked Strong to do something similar in the thirty acre grounds of his Windsor home.

'I've always loved gardens and I've always loved flowers,' Elton told Caroline Cass 'In the house where I was born in Pinner Hill Road, we had a beautiful garden and we always had a mass of flowers in the house throughout my childhood. Even though the gardens of my youth were small and suburban, they were invariably pretty. As a kid, you're always made to mow the lawn. I didn't mind mowing, but weeding I hated.'

Luckily, now that Elton is one of the richest men in Britain with an estimated fortune in excess of £150 million, he no longer has to do his own weeding, and 'small' and 'suburban' are two more things he has long left behind.

Today his garden at Woodside boasts two stone lions, each weighing six tons – and a city tram which he bought and shipped back to Britain while on tour in Melbourne.

Elton may be embarking on his sixth decade in a more sober fashion, but in 1997 any worries that he might be about to retreat permanently into the potting shed were banished on the occasion of his 50th birthday party when he proved that he had lost none of his outlandish sense of fun. Over 600 of his nearest and dearest gathered to celebrate at the Hammersmith Palais, all in lavish fancy dress. But even hardened Elton-watchers were left speechless by the birthday boy's own entrance. He was dressed in an outrageous gravity-defying concoction – so extravagantly large that he had to be delivered to the star-studded party in the back of a furniture van. As he was lowered gently to the ground on a hydraulic tail-lift, it became apparent that Elton had come as Louis XIV, the Sun King.

As he made his magnificent way through the waiting crowd, the enormous silver wig perched precariously, complete with pirate ship and canons; and a 20 foot train of ostrich feathers trailing in his wake, the world breathed a collective sigh of relief. Even in the notoriously beige 1990s, there was no evidence that Elton John had any intention of starting to take himself seriously, or indeed of growing old that gracefully. **ej**

*Elton with his manager John Reid – the
duo split in May 1998 after one of the
longest artiste-manager relationships in
the music business*

David Furnish, Elton and Princess Diana at the funeral of their mutual friend, fashion designer Gianni Versace

Candle In The Wind

Not all Elton's spending is frivolous. He also has an eye to more permanent investments, inspired perhaps by his mother. 'She always wanted me to put money into bricks and mortar,' he once said. 'I'm addicted to buying a piece of property, doing it up and then buying another piece.' At present, Elton's properties include a Chelsea Harbour penthouse, his Windsor mansion and the recently purchased Castel Mont Alban just outside Nice in the South of France. It was here in May 1998 that he hosted the latest in a long line of star-studded celebrity parties. Even by Elton's standards, the celebratory dinner he held to coincide with the 51st Cannes Film Festival was lavish.

The event was held to alert the film world to the existence of Elton and David Furnish's Rocket Films and the three films the company currently has in development: a comedy set in Edinburgh; a biography of Somalian model Waris Dirie; and *In God's Name*, a thriller set in the Vatican. The guest-list included Mr and Mrs Ringo Starr, Sigourney Weaver, Farrah

Fawcett, Steve Buscemi, Stanley Tucci, Lena Olin, director Alan Parker, Beatrice Dalle and Sharon Stone, who had earlier grabbed all the Cannes headlines. At an AIDS benefit held at the end of the festival, the actress 'auctioned' herself off for £28,000 and then danced along to Elton's performances of 'Twist and Shout' and 'Great Balls Of Fire'.

Although Elton's zest for life and luxury appears undiminished, there does seem to be a sense of proportion and balance which was missing from his life before. 'There's an inner peace now,' he says, 'but there are times when that inner peace is rattled and I become the dark, broody, unhappy person I was before. Recovery is a never-ending process. Those demons that will always be inside me sometimes rear their ugly head. But they usually don't win any more.'

Throughout all the turmoil and crises of Elton's very public life his fans never lost faith, a fact which he acknowledges gratefully: 'Audiences have always been very kind to me – very generous and very warm – and I never knew how to respond to that. I was always embarrassed by it, I didn't know how to accept praise.' But if there had been any doubt about the enormous groundswell of public affection for the short, bespectacled, be-weaved performer, it was swept away decisively on the morning of 6 September 1997, when Elton John sat down nervously behind a piano in Westminster Abbey and sang 'Candle In The Wind' at the funeral service for his friend Diana, Princess of Wales.

'Candle In The Wind' was already established as one of his most popular songs and it had long been among Elton's personal favourites. The lyrics had even given Bernie Taupin an entry in the *Penguin Dictionary of 20th Century Quotations*. "Candle In The Wind' is the best song we've ever written,' Bernie told *Rolling Stone* in 1973. 'It's my favourite song, it means a lot to me. The sentiment is how I feel, and the melody really suits the mood of it. It may come across as another schmaltzy song, but people can listen to it and realise what the writers feel for her.'

Following Diana's death and the news that Elton John had been asked to perform at her Funeral, the choice of song seemed far from straightforward. Neither 'Your Song' nor 'Don't Let The Sun Go Down On Me' seemed apt, and the lyrics of the original 'Candle In The Wind' were patently inappropriate. Writing a new song was always a possibility, but even for such seasoned writers, composing to order and

against a deadline is always a fraught business. In the end they decided on an adaptation and, to his eternal credit, in less than an hour Bernie Taupin came up with a set of new and more fitting lyrics for the much loved song.

So much has been written about the death of Diana and its immediate aftermath, but it is still impossible to convey to anyone not in the country at the time the full impact of that strange week. Diana was the most famous woman in the world; and to many who were weary of the fustiness of the royal family, she had come as a breath of fresh air. Even those who were less enamoured could not help but watch fascinated as the drama of her life unfolded, day by day, before our very eyes. There was something almost Shakespearean in the way she cut a swathe through the stubborn traditions of a royal household made rigid by generations of complacency.

Blushing deeply, she had moved modestly, almost reluctantly into the royal frame; but before long she was upstaging them all. Within a few years, the '80s had become the Decade of Diana and she seemed – even to quite rational observers – to offer The House of Windsor its only real hope of survival. And then came the inevitable divorce and the growing realisation at court that their saviour had become their nemesis. By the time of the *Panorama* interview in November 1995, she was well on the road to overturning the

*A reminder of more carefree days:
the clown and the biker – Elton in
performance with George Michael*

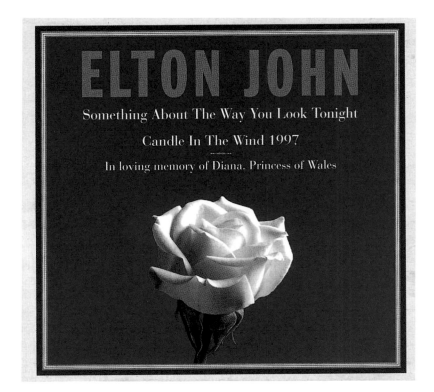

monarchy, and with it centuries of tradition. It now seemed that for Diana anything was possible – anything, except that within two short years she would be gone.

Diana's death affected people from all walks of life: from the old guard who mourned her loss as they would mourn any member of the royal family, to the disaffected whom she had met and championed. She was missed by the young, the disabled, the ethnic minorities, the gay community, the *Country Life* set… It was just hard to imagine a world without her. Her passing made a real impact precisely because her life had been so public. We had

seen her first as a shy teenager and had followed her progress through nanny to royal wife and mother, fashion icon, style-setter. We had read of her marital unhappiness, heard of the bulimia…and all the while, she was there on every front page and almost every nightly news, looking young and beautiful and vital.

The British television audience for the funeral at Westminster Abbey was made up of over 31 million people. Worldwide, Elton was singing to an audience estimated to have exceeded two billion. There are others who could have done what Elton John did in Westminster Abbey: George Michael; Sting;

Paul McCartney; all would have made a decent fist of whatever tribute they chose. But it is hard to imagine any of them making quite the impact that the cuddly but strangely dignified presence of Elton John did that day.

Not everyone was entranced though. The Reverend Neil Ross of the Free Presbyterian Church of Scotland attacked Elton's inclusion in the service on the grounds that his 'immorality is public knowledge'. He also found 'offensive' the use of such a 'worldly' pop song, 'such is the spiritual darkness that pervades the country that the singer was centre-stage during the funeral.'

Elton has vowed never to perform the re-written song in public again. It was a fitting testament to the memory of his friend; and it is fitting that our only souvenir of that hauntingly simple performance will be the memory of a brave man, fighting back the tears, as he poured his heart into the performance of a lifetime. A recording of the song was, however, inevitable. Straight from the Abbey, Elton went to Chiswick's Townhouse Studios, where Sir George Martin had agreed to produce a version of 'Candle In The Wind 1997' for release as a single. Sir George had already announced his retirement and this was to be his final record production. After a legendary career lasting nearly half a century, during which he had steered the likes of Bernard Cribbins, Peter Sellers and The Beatles to chart glory, the unforgettable swansong would be Elton's tribute to Diana.

Discs began to be pressed early in the morning of 8 September, barely 48 hours after Elton's performance at Westminster Abbey. Such was the expected demand that copies of 'Candle In The Wind 1997' were being produced not only in the UK, but also in Germany, France and Holland. The first consignments arrived on the morning of September 12, and the next day saw it selling more copies in a single day than any previous release. A record 658,000 units had been sold by the end of Saturday and the following day 'Candle In The Wind 1997' reached No.1 as the UK's fastest-selling single ever.

With the trauma of Diana's death still fresh in the nation's mind, 'Candle In The Wind 1997' took on a life of its own and the momentum propelled it into the record books. It became the first single ever to be certified quadruple platinum. In *Music Week*, Alan Jones wrote: 'Having topped a million sales in five days – more than halving the eleven days required by the previous record-holder Band Aid's 'Do They Know It's Christmas' – it has actually accelerated and, by close of business on Saturday, had sold an estimated 2,205,000 copies. It outsold the No.2 by a margin of 18 to one and accounted for a remarkable 58% of the total singles market.' Elsewhere the magazine calculated that if all the copies of the single sold were stacked on top of each other, they would measure the equivalent of

277 Nelson's Columns.

The global impact was equally astonishing. In Canada, advance orders for 'Candle In The Wind' reached 600,000 – extraordinary given the fact that no single in that country had ever sold more than 350,000. The song reached No.1 in France, Germany, Holland, Switzerland, Sweden, Austria, Spain, Ireland, Belgium, Norway, Italy, America and Israel – the country's first-ever gold single.

The media tried hard to build Elton's friendship with Diana into more than it actually was. The two met frequently at charity functions and worked to support each other's causes, but a rift developed between them when, on the advice of Buckingham Palace, Diana withdrew a foreword she had written for a book, *Rock and Royalty*, the proceeds of which had been pledged to Elton's AIDS Foundation. A very public and very tearful reunion took place at the funeral of Gianni Versace, where Diana was photographed comforting Elton, who was utterly distraught at the shocking and senseless murder in Miami of his Italian friend.

Certainly Diana and Elton knew each other and she was known to enjoy his music, but their main point of contact was their well-publicised shared interest in AIDS. As a gay man who had been sexually active during the 1970s and '80s – he admitted his sexual promiscuity at the time was largely unprotected – Elton felt himself lucky to have escaped the virus. However while he himself remained in the clear, the death of Ryan White had brought him to his senses, shocking him sufficiently to propel him into therapy. Since this de-toxing in the late '80s, Elton has ensured that the proceeds of every subsequent single have gone towards his vital and tireless crusade to help AIDS sufferers.

Elton's new album *The Big Picture* had long been scheduled for release on 29 September 1997, to be preceded by the single 'Something About The Way You Look Tonight'. Now though, suggestions were rife that the album was being rushed out to cash-in on the success of 'Candle In The Wind'. In fact, the release of a new album by a star of Elton's stature is planned not unlike a military operation: every territory must be serviced with singles and videos, print and television interviews, live performances and prestige showcases. Logistics dictate that the launch of any new 'product' must be strategically planned months ahead. From the point of view of concentrating efforts on the new album, the 'Candle In The Wind' juggernaut could hardly have come at a worse time for Elton. The criticisms were inevitable, echoing those Bob Geldof had attracted 14 years before, when it was suggested that the whole Band Aid phenomenon had been simply a last desperate attempt to re-activate his failing career.

Late in September 'Candle In The Wind' was still selling an estimated 200,000 copies a day in the UK, and on the eve of its US release,

*A distraught Elton after singing
'Candle In The Wind 1997' at
Princess Diana's funeral*

advance orders were in the region of four million. The American release was accompanied by a level of hysteria unseen since the heyday of Beatlemania. It became only the seventh single ever to debut at No.1 in the half century history of the American singles charts – and the first by a British act.

By the first week in October, 'Candle In The Wind' had overtaken 'Do They Know It's Christmas' to become the UK's best-selling single ever. At the same time it overtook The Beatles' 'I Want To Hold Your Hand' as the most successful single by a British artist. It was eventually pushed off the UK No.1 spot on 25 October, by The Spice Girls' 'Spice Up Your Life'. By then, 'Candle In The Wind 1997' was safely in the record books as the best-selling single ever released, with sales well in excess of 33 million copies.

In the weeks following the chart domination of 'Candle In The Wind', *New Musical Express* was full of anti-Elton propaganda. The *NME* of 20 September 1997 ran a full-page feature headlined 'Stop The Madness. Why 'Candle In The Wind' Is The Death Of Rock'. Despite having featured Elton prominently on their cover in 1994, *NME*'s attitude was typically brattish and confrontational, snapping at the heels of the single's success and bitching that Elton had kept The Verve's 'The Drugs Don't Work' off the top. Of course, *NME* had to be in-yer-face and rock 'n' roll about it all. After all it's their job to promote The Verve and Asian Dub Foundation. And Elton John, when it suits them.

On tour to promote *The Big Picture* – shows which took place while the memory of Elton seated at the piano in the Abbey was still vivid and the world's best-selling single was still being played almost constantly – Elton acknowledged the gap in the programme caused by the omission of 'Candle In The Wind' and instead took to performing a song called 'Sand And Water' by the American singer-songwriter Beth Neilsen Chapman. The song had been written for Chapman's husband who died of cancer in 1994, and when Elton first heard it, he felt it reflected his sense of loss at the deaths of Diana and Versace. 'It says everything I want to say,' Elton told the *Los Angeles Times*. 'I can't sing 'Candle In The Wind', but I have to get something out of me and that song will help me do it.'

'Candle In The Wind 1997' will always remain inextricably linked with the death of Diana. Many people are still disturbed by how intensely they felt the death of this young woman whom few had even met. But at the time, Elton John's performance caught precisely the mood of a nation still reeling from the shock. While the words of the Poet Laureate were appreciated, the feeling was that it was Bernie Taupin's words, as sung by his long-time partner, which best captured the mood of the moment.

In an interview in 1986, Elton had spoken of his delight at being asked to Prince Andrew's wedding, adding in words which would find tragic echo a decade later: 'I love churches, because the music always sounds wonderful.'

It was in that same church, eleven years on, that the UK's best-loved entertainer reached out to his largest-ever audience and felt that audience reaching back to him with love and affection. **ej**

Elton: The Music I

Denmark Street is a tiny London byway. It cuts through just by the base of Tottenham Court Road, almost buried by Centre Point, one of London's first and best-known skyscrapers. On the other side of Charing Cross Road lies bohemian Soho, but Denmark Street is on the business side of the street, the place where all the deals are done.

It was to that short, undistinguished stretch of street that Reg Dwight made the daily journey from Pinner in Middlesex – to the premises of Mills Music, where he worked as

tea boy in his first job after leaving school. For as long as there was popular music, Denmark Street had been the capital's Tin Pan Alley, a cynosure for songwriters, music publishers and agents. It was the place where all musical goods were peddled: songs to managers; rights to publishers; and equipment to musicians. The deals made here in the early days of pop would resonate for decades to come. Those hasty, back-of-an-envelope, sealed-with-a-handshake agreements effectively laying the foundations for the multi-billion pound industry

which grew up over the next 30 years.

The hub of the music industry, Denmark Street was where the music publishers clustered. Before The Beatles introduced the rather radical concept of bands providing their own songs, this was where all the decisions were made – by middle-aged men from the old school of showbusiness. Al Stewart remembers spending an entire day following Paul Simon along Denmark Street, as the young American desperately tried to flog off his song catalogue (which already included 'Homeward Bound'

and 'Sound Of Silence') to uninterested publishers for a paltry £5,000.

The tidal wave of Beatlemania – and the shocking news that the group was a self-contained unit with no need of outside assistance – caused dismay in the cafes and tiny offices of Tin Pan Alley. The growing popularity of Bob Dylan was even more worrying. Dylan was literally a one-man band. He wrote and recorded all his own material, thereby completely obviating the need for professional song publishers. With his

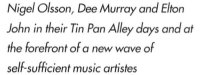

Nigel Olsson, Dee Murray and Elton John in their Tin Pan Alley days and at the forefront of a new wave of self-sufficient music artistes

corrosive voice and his own songs, Dylan posed a real threat – he proved that anyone could do it. It wasn't so much what Dylan said that was concerning, but the fact that he said it all by himself.

Much to the chagrin of the established music-men, The Beatles soon looked set to re-write the pop rulebook. For within their ranks lay concealed a vital secret weapon: a pair of seamless pop craftsmen. Without the songwriting team of John Lennon and Paul

McCartney, it is conceivable that The Beatles' success may have been as quickfire as that of Liverpool contemporaries like The Searchers, The Swinging Blue Jeans and The Fourmost – all good groups, more than capable of performing the latest pop, rock 'n' roll and R&B hits – but unable to sustain a whole career on covers alone.

During the '60s the old mould was finally broken and a new order emerged, ushering in a whole new era of British pop music. But it was

Lennon and McCartney who first kicked down the doors of Tin Pan Alley and left them open for the generation of singer-songwriters who followed. Al Stewart and Cat Stevens, Nick Drake and Richard Thompson, Elton John and Bernie Taupin – all certainly had much to thank them for.

A teaboy at Mills Music by day, at night Reg Dwight was already moonlighting with Bluesology. But it was during his days on Tin Pan Alley that Elton forged musical friendships which would endure for much of his early career – with Dick James, promoter Vic Lewis and guitarist Caleb Quaye. Agreements made back then would eventually come back to haunt Elton, when in 1985 he sued Dick James over songwriting copyrights which had initially been traded in and around Denmark Street. But although there may have been regrets later on, it was here in the heart of Soho that the real story of Elton John and his music begins.

The early singles with Bluesology were unremarkable efforts. It was only after making his way symbolically to Mayfair's Albemarle Street and the offices of Liberty Records that Reg began to make the musical transition into Elton John. And crucially, it was not until he began writing in tandem with Bernie Taupin that there was any real indication of a sustainable songwriting career.

Elton and Bernie were both self-confessed musical sponges: two avid record-buyers who were keen to listen to everything and happy to soak up anything. So obvious was the influence on their work of whatever else was around in the pop climate of the period, that you can tell just by the titles of a couple of unreleased collaborations exactly when they were written. 'Tartan Coloured Lady', 'When I Was Tealby Abbey' and 'Regimental Sergeant Zippo' for example, all date from 1968, the post-*Sgt Pepper* year when every English songwriter was trying to match The Beatles' magical blend of lyrical other-worldliness and psychedelic music hall.

Elton's first solo single, 'I've Been Loving You', was released in March 1968, a big ballad in the style of the then-popular Engelbert Humperdinck, Tom Jones, Solomon King and Long John Baldry. Though credited to Elton John/Bernie Taupin, this was in fact an Elton solo composition. Bernie remembered later that although Elton had written it without his help, 'he felt guilty and, because we'd been working so much together, he felt I deserved credit.'

Their facility for absorbing all kinds of musical influences served Elton and Bernie well in the beginning. And although they started by sounding like whoever else was around – Leonard Cohen, Traffic, The Band – they soon began to develop their own distinctive musical style. It was a sound powered along by well-played piano, which showcased Elton's bluesy vocals while bringing out the best in Bernie's frequently inscrutable but always highly atmospheric lyrics.

Sweat, stacks and spangly slacks –
Elton stomps out another
bluesy number

At the end of the 1960s though, you would still have been hard pushed to find anyone ready to put money on Elton John as being 'the next big thing'. There was certainly a talent, but there was also a lot of stiff competition. When Elton's debut solo album *Empty Sky* was released in June 1969, The Beatles were still holding together as a group, Bob Dylan was in the ascendant and the Rolling Stones were invariably cited as 'the world's greatest rock 'n' roll band'.

In January 1969 *New Musical Express* had reviewed Elton's new single 'Lady Samantha' favourably, calling it 'professional and musicianly', but the record made no impact whatsoever on the charts and a few months later *Empty Sky* struggled to sell more than 4,000 copies. Not surprisingly though, Elton retains the greatest fondness for that very first album: 'Making the *Empty Sky* album still holds the nicest memories for me, because it was the first, I suppose. It's difficult to explain the amazement we felt as the album began to take shape. But I remember when we finished work on the title track – it just floored me. I thought it was the best thing I'd ever heard in my life.'

Within a year there was a second album in the shops, this one simply entitled *Elton John*. To promote its release in April 1970, Elton, together with drummer Nigel Olsson and bassist Dee Murray (both previously in the post-Steve Winwood Spencer Davis group), made

his debut at London's Roundhouse, supporting Marc Bolan's duo – the still acoustic Tyrannosaurus Rex. A little later in the year they appeared again at the same venue, this time playing support to Sandy Denny's sadly short-lived Fotheringay. It was all part of an invaluable musical apprenticeship and the three men would continue playing together for some years. In 1971, they were joined by guitarist Davey Johnstone from the folk group Magna Carta, who plays with Elton to this day.

Slowly, gradually, as the new decade got under way, Elton John began to make an impression. Watching *Top Of The Pops* during April 1970, *Melody Maker*'s Richard Williams was struck by the sight of 'a slight youth seated at a grand piano singing and playing an amazing God Rock ballad which quite put the insipid 'Let It Be' into true perspective. The song was called 'Border Song' and the singer was Elton John.'

Even this early in his career, critics were staggered by Elton's prolificity and it is now believed that in March 1970, Elton had made an agreement with Dick James Music which obliged him to provide six sides of original music per annum, rather than the more standard four. This meant that between 1970 and 1975, Elton John was committed to writing, recording and promoting no fewer than three albums of original material every year. In fact he didn't quite meet this target. Even if you count *Goodbye Yellow Brick Road*

as two and include the live set and the film soundtrack, the grand total comes to just 13 albums during the period. But even ignoring the almost unparalleled hit rate, this is an incredible achievement. In just ten months leading up to his January 1971 breakthrough with 'Your Song', Elton had managed to release the classy 'Border Song' and 'Rock & Roll Madonna' as singles, as well as a pair of thoroughly assured albums, *Elton John* and *Tumbleweed Connection*.

It was *Elton John* (the album) that finally made Elton John (the man) into ELTON JOHN (the star). Because he has become such a familiar figure over the past 30 years, it is hard now to remember that the young man pictured on the cover of that landmark album was once completely unknown. While it may be fanciful to suggest that the sleeve was intended to recall the shadowy figures of the Fab Four on *With The Beatles* seven years before, it does convey a similar sense of mystery. There is nothing but a portrait, a pale white face emerging from darkness. Quite ageless. And a name – but what sort of name was 'Elton'? Had to be American…

Once past the curious cover, there was a quiet perfection to the songs within. Particularly the outstanding 'Your Song', 'Take Me To The Pilot', 'First Episode At Hienton', 'Sixty Years On', 'Border Song' and 'The King Must Die'. A 60% hit rate. Which, at the time, was a good deal better than David Bowie, Crosby, Stills & Nash, or Paul McCartney were managing.

Elton in the days of his eponymous breakthrough album (opposite) — already the trademark glasses were in place

The vocal style too was instantly engaging: already a swampy, soulful singer, Elton's voice was further enhanced by Paul Buckmaster's florid orchestrations. However such rich arrangements quickly swallowed up the album's limited budget: 'The first big budget album I was allowed to make,' Elton told *Mojo's* Cliff Jones. 'We're talking about a budget of £7,000 – you could get a semi in Pinner for that. I had the very best – Trident Studios, an arranger, Gus Dudgeon and orchestra. We were going to get George Martin but we already had Paul Buckmaster, a genius who did the strings on 'Space Oddity'. Most of the cash went on the orchestra actually – we had to record three songs per session because they cost so much. Absolutely fucking terrifying!'

Versatility and variety were the order of the day in 1970. Not content with kicking over the traces of the '60s, rock 'n' roll was moving forward decisively to meet the new decade:

and in that brave new world, progressive rock ruled. With hindsight, the pretentiousness and bombast are witheringly embarrassing, but at the time, lengthy drum solos, lavish orchestrations and impressionistic lyrics were undeniably the order of the day.

The one element of Elton's eponymous 1970 album which now sounds particularly dated, is the lushness of the orchestrations – which at the time seemed so impressive. Otherwise, Elton hits out for six in all directions: the bedsit balladry of 'Your Song'; the poignancy of 'First Episode At Hienton' and 'Sixty Years On'; and the slow, smouldering funk of 'Border Song'…all helped to indicate that this album marked the arrival of a potent new star for the 1970s.

On its release the album was reviewed enthusiastically in both *New Musical Express* and *Melody Maker*. The latter's Richard Williams taking a particular shine to Elton, which was important as *Melody Maker* – with weekly sales in the region of 120,000 – was a virtual Bible for anyone remotely interested in rock music in the British Isles during the early 1970s. *Elton John* sold an estimated 12,000 copies, three times as many as *Empty Sky* and sufficient to gain Elton John his first-ever chart placing.

The album eventually reached No.11 on the UK charts, but neither 'Border Song' nor

'Rock & Roll Madonna' made it into the singles chart. As 1970 drew on, Elton John remained very much a cult act, more a part of the thriving underground than the populist overground. Elton was now playing frequently at happening haunts like the Roundhouse, the Country Club, the Lyceum and the Marquee. The word was gradually getting out, but it was a slow-burn and largely London-based. It was not until he left these shores for the first time, in the summer of 1970, that things really started hotting up for Elton John.

In 1970 *Melody Maker* ran the headline: 'Dylan Digs Elton.' The paper went on to report that Bob Dylan, then rarely seen in public, had made the journey across to New York's Fillmore East and dug the new singing sensation out of England. In fact, Dylan had gone along to check out Leon Russell (who later enjoyed a short-lived spell as his producer) – but Dylan was gracious enough to the new kids on the block.

Bernie would later recall that: 'The high point of the first couple of tours was Dylan coming to the Fillmore. I didn't even recognise him. Elton said, "This is Bob Dylan." I wasn't really ready for it, what can I say? I mean, it was like, "Oh God!", or "You're God!"' (Bernie's mother remembered that on another occasion, when he and Elton went to see Bob Dylan on the Isle of Wight, they had sent her a postcard saying, 'We've been to see God.') But today Taupin is able to remain a little more

composed: 'I can walk into a room with him and not collapse in a babbling wreck on the floor. I can sit down and talk about basketball with him.'

One of the engaging features that Elton and Bernie have in common is that throughout their years of fame they have retained a sense of awe and delight at meeting their musical heroes. That first trip to America during the summer of 1970 saw Elton John headlining at the prestigious Troubadour Club in Los Angeles; and from early on, it was apparent that Elton was out to conquer. The reviews which greeted his initial shows were ecstatic. Critics delighted in his introspective, finely-crafted ballads and revelled in the moments of Jerry Lee Lewis-style rock 'n' roll abandon when he kicked the piano stool away and let rip. But for Elton, the joy of his first trip outside Britain was diluted by the fact that his name appeared bigger than that of David Ackles, his fellow piano-playing troubadour. Ackles was an artist whom both he and Bernie admired tremendously – Elton's next album *Tumbleweed Connection* was dedicated to the American singer-songwriter and Bernie went on to produce Ackles' acclaimed 1972 album *American Gothic*.

The two Englishmen abroad could hardly believe their luck when American legends like Brian Wilson, The Band and Al Kooper – previously familiar only from their album sleeves – began queuing up to shake hands. And for Elton, his first visit to LA's massive Tower

Records store was almost as thrilling as a headlining stint at the Troubadour. A London friend can remember his surprise when an excited Elton rang from America to gloat that he had just bought a copy of Neil Young's new album *After The Goldrush*.

Elton's conquest of America came in the first year of the new decade, when The Beatles were just beginning their public and protracted break-up; the Stones were in retreat after the tragedy at Altamont in December 1969; and Bob Dylan was still licking his wounds from the mauling *Self Portrait* had received at the hands of the critics. The likes of Bruce Springsteen, David Bowie and Marc Bolan were all waiting in the wings, serving their apprenticeships in folk clubs and small halls, or as opening acts. But the time was without doubt ripe for something and someone new.

According to Elton's American A&R man Russ Regan, a promotional budget of $20,000 was all it took to break Elton John in the States in 1970. It was Regan who persuaded Elton's American labelmate Neil Diamond to introduce the new British name at the Troubadour. On that first night a fair number of the audience probably turned up because they had heard it was a Neil Diamond concert. But by the end of the evening, few were in any doubt as to who was the star of the show.

Elton later recalled that the Troubadour show 'was the first time I knew something really big was happening, that was really when I became Elton. I mean, I was Elton before that, but that was when I really launched into Elton John.' **ej**

Early in his career Elton had to learn to perform to huge crowds – a training that stood him in good stead for the stadium audiences he regularly plays to now

Elton: The Music II

The one that really got the critics sitting up and taking notice was Elton's third album, *Tumbleweed Connection*, which was released in the autumn of 1970. Tapping into Bernie Taupin's well-documented fascination with the Old West, the album delighted British critics still under the influence of their first intoxicating exposure to the music of The Band.

It is hard to credit nowadays just how mysterious and legendary The Band seemed during 1970. They had appeared out of nowhere (well, Canada actually) to back Bob

Dylan on his controversial 1966 world tour, during which he was loudly booed for his efforts at going electric. Then the following year they withdrew – again with Bob – to the basement of a house called Big Pink, situated in the tiny artistic hamlet of Woodstock, in upstate New York. It was here that the now legendary *Basement Tapes* first saw the light of day. Later they would provide the source material for rock 'n' roll's first-ever bootleg album.

When it came out in 1968, The Band's own debut album *Music From Big Pink* was, for

many, the album of the year. Eric Clapton, George Harrison and Richard Thompson were just some of those singing its praises. And things only got better with their second album *The Band* in 1969. Staring sombrely from its brown-bordered cover, The Band were clearly men to reckon with, rugged veterans of the rock 'n' roll wars, taking time out amidst the Arcadian beauty of Woodstock, at least until later that year when the festival made their presence no longer tenable. By the time they came to make their UK concert debut,

headlining at the Royal Albert Hall in 1970, the anticipation was tangible.

The Band had already cast their long shadows all over *Tumbleweed Connection*, and such was Elton and Bernie's indebtedness that they wrote the song 'Levon' for their next album *Madman Across The Water*, as a tribute to Levon Helm – The Band's singing drummer. From the suburban room they still shared in Pinner, Elton and Bernie tried as best they could to convey the space, mystery and myth of the American West. From its cover on in,

Tumbleweed Connection had the atmosphere of the American Wild West. Elton's shows, on the other hand, were more Las Vegas glitz

Tumbleweed Connection evoked the spirit of American frontier life. The beautifully-packaged album came lavishly illustrated with old prints of six-guns, Mississippi steamboats and iron horses. The opening track, 'Ballad Of A Well-Known Gun', was self-evident – but other songs, 'Country Comfort', 'My Father's Gun', 'Son Of Your Father' and 'Burn Down The Mission' also spoke of Bernie Taupin's fascination with a life he could only dream of.

Strange as it may seem, *Tumbleweed Connection* was more or less complete before the two young men even left the country. As Bernie explained: 'Everybody thinks that I was influenced by Americana and seeing America first hand, but we wrote and recorded the album before we'd even been to the States. It was totally influenced by The Band's album *Music From Big Pink* and Robbie Robertson's songs. I've always loved Americana and I love American westerns. I've always said that 'El Paso' (by Marty Robbins) was the song that made me want to write songs. It was the perfect meshing of melody and storyline.'

The atmosphere of *Tumbleweed Connection* was inspired by John Wayne and Gary Cooper; a world informed by repeated Sunday afternoon viewings of *High Noon*, *Shane*, *Stagecoach* and *My Darling Clementine*. Bernie's words had life breathed into them by Elton's fervent vocals, which on this album still sound as though they could have been forged on a cotton plantation somewhere south of the Mason-Dixon line. This third album was arguably Elton's finest ever. But incredibly, although it contains some superlative examples

both of Elton's music and Bernie's lyrics, it didn't yield a single hit. While the western frontier obsession may seem rather naïve now, the record was suffused with a genuinely infectious enthusiasm for a country which, at the time it was made, the two had yet to see. This is Elton and Bernie's take on the pioneering days of the Wild West, as viewed from the Northwood Hills in Middlesex. The actuality could never even begin to live up to their imaginings.

Tumbleweed Connection is chock full of striking songs – the driving and atmospheric 'Ballad Of A Well-Known Gun', the gospel fire of 'Where To Now St Peter?' and 'Burn Down The Mission'. But best of all is 'Country Comfort', a rocking, rolling slice of Americana, topped off with one of Elton's most memorable melodies. Rod Stewart recognised the inherent

quality of the song and included it on his contemporaneous album *Gasoline Alley*, while at the same time forging one of rock music's more unlikely friendships. Rod the striking, swaggering, absurdly red-blooded, overtly heterosexual rock 'n' roller; and Elton, the shy, sensitive homosexual. But they shared a passion for football and music and the high life, and somehow the friendship has endured.

On its release in October 1970, *Tumbleweed Connection* reached a respectable No.6 in the album charts. The critics were enthusiastic about the way that Elton and Bernie had hijacked American music and made it their own and as the first year of the new decade began to wind down, Elton John was established as a cult favourite – hailed by the weekly music press, popular with students and

Not usually a publicity-shy performer, Marc Bolan's piano-hideaway would never last

championed by DJ John Peel. But everything was set to change with the release of an old song as Elton's first single of 1971.

Fans were surprised when they purchased Elton John's current album *Tumbleweed Connection*, to find that it didn't contain the hit single 'Your Song', which had reached No.7 late in January 1971. This was the single which began Elton's incredible, unbroken run of chart success. It is Elton's 'Yesterday', his 'Just The Way You Are', his 'Knockin' On Heaven's Door'... Not necessarily the composers' best songs, nor even their best-loved compositions, but for legions of fans the defining moment.

'Your Song' opened the doors on an extraordinarily fertile period, which saw Elton John dominating the charts on both sides of the Atlantic, from the time of its release until 1976. It was also his first American hit, reaching No.8 late in 1970, and in the absence of The Beatles giving him a free run in the area of British occupation of the American charts. He was enjoying himself too – feted by his peers wherever he went, making records he wanted to make, and then watching them get great reviews and sell in unheard-of quantities. It couldn't get much better than this.

However Elton wasn't able to fully capitalise on the success of 'Your Song'. A workaholic long before he became an alcoholic, he was committed to producing the soundtrack for an anodyne film called *Friends*, which was intended to cash-in on the success of *Love Story*. He was also touring intensively in both the UK and America, and by January 1971 was having to cancel dates as a result of exhaustion. The venues had grown a lot bigger since his days at the Roundhouse – he was now easily capable of filling London's Royal Festival Hall or the Anaheim Convention Center in Los Angeles.

Incredibly, the quality of the music didn't seem to suffer from the intense pressure under which Elton was operating. The obligatory live album *17-11-70* had been followed by the *Friends* soundtrack, but *Madman Across The Water* was the first proper album since the success of 'Your Song'. Whilst not in the same league as *Tumbleweed Connection*, *Madman Across The Water* nonetheless had much to recommend it – not least the opening track 'Tiny Dancer', an affectionate portrait of Los Angeles and Bernie's new wife Maxine. 'Levon' was a New York inspired gospel piece, while the title track had all the epic sweep and scope of Elton at his best. Another track which attracted a lot of interest was 'All The Nasties', a none too veiled swipe at the critics.

'I was very sensitive to criticism,' Elton admitted later. 'After being the darling boy of the radio and critics for the first two years of your career, things took a turn. I now understand that's a natural process, but I always wanted everything to be wonderful and of course it isn't. I've given up reading the critics. I don't read music papers anymore, I've outgrown them.'

The critics sniped and Elton sulked, but the hits just kept on a-comin'. These really were the glory years: a whole string of songs which were to provide Elton with the foundations of his career, sprang out of the traps and straight up the charts. In April 1972 when Britain was in the grip of T.Rexstasy, 'Rocket Man' was kept off the No.1 slot by Marc Bolan's 'Metal Guru'; but 'Honky Cat', 'Crocodile Rock', 'Daniel', 'Saturday Night's Alright For Fighting' and 'Goodbye Yellow Brick Road' were all British hits during the 12 months from September 1972 until September 1973. In America though, Elton's complete conquest of the charts would have to wait for another year or so.

Elton John would eventually straddle the American charts like a Colossus during the mid-'70s. The fans bought the music in such quantities that Elton entered the record books again with virtually every release. But it wasn't just the music which impressed them. There was something larger than life which appealed particularly to the Americans; and in performance, Elton was only too delighted to keep bettering himself.

'I remember going to see Guy Mitchell once at the London Palladium,' Elton told music author Joe Smith. 'At the end of his set, he took his sock off and whirled it around his head. I thought "what a funny guy." I never forgot that, and maybe that accounts for why I would get

so outrageous on stage. I've done talk shows in England and they'd like it if I came on in an angel outfit. It's OK for the stage, but when you're sitting down talking to someone you feel a bit of a prat. I never thought the outfits got in the way of the music. I did live my teenage years through my success years in my twenties. I never had the freedom to do that before, so I did it. With me, I'm afraid, I'm very excessive. If I do it, I do it to the extreme.'

However it took more than a man with silly glasses, tottering on unfeasibly high platform soles and dressed as Donald Duck, to account for the fact that in America at his peak, an astonishing 3% of all records sold were by Elton John. The music was listener-friendly: Led Zeppelin were simultaneously conquering America, but their music was specifically aimed at a generation too young for the Rolling Stones. Elton John though had the potential to appeal to everyone from six to sixty – a record company's dream constituency.

Honky Chateau in May 1972 is remembered chiefly for the hit singles 'Honky Cat' and 'Rocket Man', but it also contained one of Elton and Bernie's best ever collaborations – 'Mona Lisas And Mad Hatters'. This was another American-inspired piece, drawn from the same well as the best of the songs on *Tumbleweed Connection*. But rather than America's western frontiers, 'Mona Lisas...' takes its cue from impressions of New York, tipping a lyrical hat to Leiber and Stoller's 'Spanish Harlem'.

Despite a positive frenzy of touring, TV performances and recording, Elton John found

The Winner from Pinner – Elton in more relaxed mode.
Even his casual clothes make a statement

time to produce not just one album to follow-up *Honky Chateau*, but two – the double *Goodbye Yellow Brick Road*. At the time, producing a double album was seen as a major statement by a major artist. Bob Dylan, The Beatles and The Rolling Stones had all released double sets prior to Elton; and *Goodbye Yellow Brick Road* was intended to show that there was more to Elton John than platform shoes and hit singles. Even if it had been little more than a vehicle for 'Candle In The Wind', *Goodbye Yellow Brick Road* would still be one of the best-loved albums in pop history. But there was a lot more to it than that.

The title track alone has a majestic, widescreen dimension – with echoes of Judy Garland, so full of promise, setting out on the golden road in *The Wizard Of Oz*. 'Bennie &

The Jets' rocks like a jukebox on a Saturday night; and 'Roy Rogers' is one of Bernie's most beautiful lyrics – a wonderfully evocative reminder of Saturday mornings at the cinema, in the days before daytime television, videos and computer games, when kids sat enchanted by the simple black and white derring-do of Roy Rogers and his trusty horse Trigger. In contrast, 'Saturday Night's Alright For Fighting' kicks in with the vigour of a skinhead's boot through the door of a hippy commune.

Inevitably, among the seventeen tracks there is some dead wood: 'Grey Seal' was originally recorded around the time of the *Elton John* album and 'Jamaica Jerk-Off' is just naff reggae – the best thing about it being the

composer credit Reggae Dwight. In the wake of the tragic death of Princess Diana, *Goodbye Yellow Brick Road* is best-known today for containing the original version of 'Candle In The Wind'. Talking to Cliff Jones in 1997, Elton admitted: 'Ask me about my favourite tracks and they will all be sad songs. A lot of my emotions come out in those sad melodies.' Indeed, one of Elton's best songs in the otherwise arid '80s was the aptly titled 'Sad Songs (Say So Much)'.

Bernie Taupin felt that the whole emphasis on a tragic identification with Marilyn Monroe was misplaced: 'The 'Candle In The Wind' thing with Marilyn Monroe was blown out of proportion because it turned everyone into thinking I was this Marilyn Monroe fanatic, but it wasn't necessarily a homage to her, it was more about misunderstanding and I've said that song could have been about James Dean.'

Surprisingly, 'Candle In The Wind' remains relatively un-covered. There have been predictably syrupy versions by Acker Bilk, Richard Clayderman and The Shadows. But one of the few versions which added any lustre to the original came courtesy of Sandy Denny on what tragically would turn out to be her final album. *Rendezvous* was released just before Sandy's premature death in 1978; ironically during 1970 Elton had frequently opened for Sandy and her band Fotheringay. In his otherwise exemplary biography *Elton*, Philip Norman describes Fotheringay's music as 'whimsical folk-rock songs about dragons, fairies and witches' spells,' which seems almost wilfully wide of the mark.

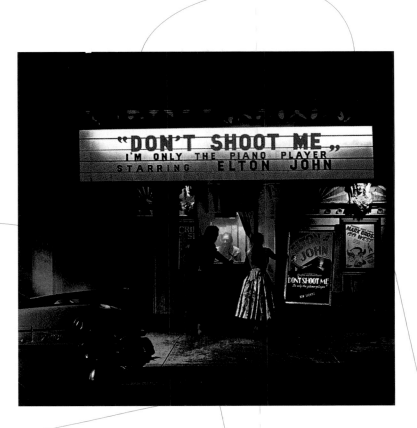

It wasn't until Elton's eighth album *Don't Shoot Me I'm Only The Piano Player* in 1973, that he scored his first UK No.1 album. Taking its title from a sign in an American saloon ('Do Not Shoot The Piano Player, He Is Doing His Best') which Oscar Wilde called the best piece of artistic criticism he had ever seen, the album lacked the broad appeal of *Goodbye Yellow Brick Road*; although it did contain two Elton classics – the elegiac 'Daniel' and the effortlessly exuberant 'Crocodile Rock'.

After four years at the top, as 1974 got under way, the strain finally began to show. Whether he felt like it or not Elton had to come up with a new album and *Caribou* was probably his least distinguished effort since *Empty Sky*. 'It was recorded under the most excruciating of circumstances,' he would recall later. 'We had eight days to do fourteen numbers. We did the backing tracks in two and a half days. It drove us crazy because there was a huge Japanese tour, then Australia and New Zealand that could not be put off. And it was the first time we'd recorded in America and we just couldn't get adjusted to the monitoring system, which was very flat. I never thought we'd get an album out of it.'

The resultant album contained at least one outstanding song: the hardy perennial 'Don't Let The Sun Go Down On Me', as well as another rarely mentioned, but creditable, track – a strangely moving soul ballad about a Northern fishing port, entitled 'Grimsby'.

But it was, in the words of former Beatle George Harrison, all too much. Something had to give. **ej**

Elton John as Captain Fantastic in the mid-1970s, pausing between hits to soak up the crowd's appreciation

Elton: The Music III

If there was a single year which marked the zenith of Elton John's American career it was 1975. That year alone he scored three No.1 American singles – a feat unheard-of since the dim and distant days of Elvis Presley or The Beatles. Meanwhile *Captain Fantastic And The Brown Dirt Cowboy* had the honour of being the first album ever to debut at the top of the American album charts. It was an incredible achievement when you consider all the albums that had gone before. And yet it was Elton John – with advance order sales of 1.4 million copies – who became the first act to go straight in at No.1. It was also the year that Elton played LA's massive Dodgers Stadium – the first act since The Beatles to do so – and he was awarded his own star on Hollywood's walk of fame. Ironically though, if 1975 was the American high point, it was also the year that marked the first indications of a decline in Elton's career at home.

After half a decade of unparalleled success, the first real cracks in the Elton John facade had begun to appear. The concept album *Captain*

Fantastic And The Brown Dirt Cowboy, though selling well, had disappointed British critics; but the real venom was reserved for Elton's show at Wembley Stadium on 21 June 1975. There had been a triumphant show at the massive venue the year before, when Crosby, Stills, Nash & Young, The Band and Joni Mitchell had all brought a little bit of West Coast magic to North London. The Stadium was only a few miles from Elton's boyhood home in Pinner, and as a youngster it had been the site of his cousin Roy Dwight's moment of glory during the 1959 FA Cup Final. Now in 1975 Elton was the star, topping a stellar, hand-picked bill which boasted The Eagles and The Beach Boys.

Elton came on as the evening sky grew dark and insisted on playing his *Captain Fantastic* album in its entirety. The new album was largely unfamiliar and the move disappointed fans who were anticipating a greatest hits package. Following a set of jukebox perfection from the world's best-loved summer band, the Beach Boys, Elton's performance seemed subdued by comparison. The show began

badly, as *Melody Maker*'s Chris Welch pointed out: 'Elton made a tactical error in starting off with the doom-laden 'Funeral For A Friend'. Tolling church bells and the sound of stark winds howling over graveyards was hardly the best way to grab the attention of the weary but willing rock fans.'

From the beginning, British fans had found the *Captain Fantastic* album a heavy concept to cope with, and anyway, by 1975 the whole idea of concept albums seemed rather outmoded. It was perhaps a sign of the times that the album was kept off the No.1 slot by a compilation – *The Best Of The Stylistics*. Elton was still effortlessly hitting the mark in America though, his Beatle-cover 'Lucy In The Sky With Diamonds' and the soul-stirring 'Philadelphia Freedom' both reached No.1 over there – but

at home they struggled to crack the Top 10. Elton John was still a superstar in Britain, though – as much for his outrageous cameo in Ken Russell's 1975 film of *Tommy* and his renowned football activities, as for his music.

Bitterly disappointed never to have scored a No.1 single in his homeland, finally in 1976 he managed it with the Kiki Dee duet 'Don't Go Breaking My Heart'. But a solo No.1 single still eluded him. And after a seamless five years at the top, where he had managed to balance powerful heart-tugging ballads with feisty rock 'n' roll, Elton John started to find himself marginalised. His split from Bernie Taupin following the release of the patchy *Blue Moves* was followed by a series of increasingly lacklustre albums. Few fans would number the albums from the late '70s – *A Single Man*,

Elton, always into the music

Dame Edna meets Sid Vicious – Elton's
stage dress has always been vibrant.
But it was the advent of riotous punk in
1976 that began to make his music
sound tired

ELTON JOHN

2
▼
4
●

TOO LOW FOR ZERO

Victim Of Love, 21 At 33, The Fox or *Jump Up* – among their Desert Island Eltons.

Elton wasn't the only one to feel the pinch. A harsh wind of Punk was blowing throughout the British music establishment during 1976-77, while America was reeling from the endless succession of boogie nights which characterised the disco boom. Punk didn't actually sell many records – but it had attitude; and the realisation grew that for the first time since The Beatles, there was a young new generation weary of what had gone before.

Once the decade's pre-eminent star, Elton John now hovered on the sidelines and watched as the '70s fizzled out. The spotlight had moved away to shine on the likes of Bruce Springsteen, Abba and David Bowie – who

had effortlessly kept one mercurial step ahead. From now on, lives would no longer be lived out to a soundtrack of Elton John albums; and even in America things had started to slide. In December 1975 he reached No.1 again with the insipid 'Island Girl' – but it would be more than twenty years before he had another solo No.1 hit in America.

The decline in his musical fortunes coincided with Elton's temporary split from long-time lyricist Bernie Taupin. Although they had never written 'nose-to-nose' – as Lennon and McCartney had when touring with The Beatles – Elton and Bernie had an innate, instinctive grasp of each other's qualities and abilities. They wrote in isolation, Elton quickly applying a melody to a set of Bernie's lyrics wherever he

happened to be at the time – on board ship, at home, in the studio…

It was a classic rock split. Both had been to the top of the mountain, and for five years – particularly in America – had looked down into the valley. There was only so long you could stay at what Lennon had called 'the toppermost of the poppermost' and for Bernie at least, that was an important contributory factor to their break-up: 'There was nowhere else to go and I just felt people must be sick of reading about us,' he said afterwards, 'I was frightened of failure. In this business there's a pinnacle you can reach, but ultimately you've got to sink down. Everybody sinks down. Everybody from the Stones to The Beatles to Springsteen.'

There were sporadic returns to the charts (the pensive instrumental 'Song For Guy' was a surprise hit in 1978), but they were one-off sorties, rather than a full-blown occupation; and any appreciation of Elton John's career from the high watermark of the mid-'70s onwards tends to major on singles rather than albums. Once reunited with Bernie Taupin in the early 1980s though, the old magic was rekindled for a couple of strong collections. *Too Low For Zero* in 1983, marked Elton and Bernie's first full collaboration in seven years – but it was a reunion in other ways too. Also on board were all the original Elton John Band members (guitarist Davey Johnstone, drummer Nigel Olsson and bassist Dee Murray – even harpist Skaila Kanga who had appeared on the *Elton John* album was brought back).

They're still standing – Elton and Bernie Taupin rekindled their writing partnership in the early '80s, putting Elton's stalled career back on track

The more subdued Elton of the '90s –
no outrageous costumes, no wild stage
antics. Just a full head of hair, classic
songs and consummate performances

Special guest Stevie Wonder helped out on the album's big hit 'I Guess That's Why They Call It The Blues', but the album also contained several other solid songs: the reflective 'Cold As Christmas'; 'Kiss The Bride'; and the punchy 'I'm Still Standing'.

In 1984 *Too Low For Zero* was followed up with *Breaking Hearts*, another strong album which contained the exuberant 'Passengers' and the poignant 'Sad Songs (Say So Much)'. But otherwise, musically the '80s wasn't a particularly distinguished decade for Elton, and albums such as *Ice On Fire*, *Leather Jackets* and *Reg Strikes Back* added little lustre to the legend. There were a couple of Top Five hits with 'Nikita' and a live 'Candle In The Wind', but largely the 1980s were the Duet Years.

Uncertain of himself, his sexuality and apparently his musical direction, Elton played strange bedfellows with an assortment of musical partners – Millie Jackson, Cliff Richard, Jennifer Rush, Aretha Franklin...

It was all predictably starry, showbiz stuff. Until in the first year of the new decade, the sea change finally came with the re-release of a nice little ballad. 'Sacrifice' hadn't aroused much interest when it was first released as a single in November 1989. In fact, it had peaked at a humiliating No.55. But DJ Steve Wright had latched onto the song tenaciously and when it was eventually re-released in June 1990, it gave Elton John his dream come true. Perhaps it was his new and passionate commitment to Aids research which gave the

Elton with long-time pal Rod Stewart –
they share a passion for football
and songs – Rod covered
Elton's 'Country Comfort'

song its keening edge. Certainly Elton had rarely sung better. And Bernie Taupin's lyrics (or 'Taupin' as he now styled himself) were right on the mark. But whatever the nature of that mysterious process which unites record-buyers, they rallied in their hundreds of thousands behind 'Sacrifice'. He had waited twenty years for it to happen, but now at last, Elton had a solo single at No.1 in the British charts.

Towards the end of 1990, on the back of 'Sacrifice', came a comprehensive double CD *The Very Best Of Elton John,* which sold and sold and sold as fans programmed their pick of every hit from 1971's 'Your Song' to 'You Gotta Love Someone' (UK No.33, 1990). Since then, the '90s have been a non-stop giddy carnival of greatest hits compilations, tribute albums, duet albums and love song packages. *Duets* in

1993 gathered together Elton's work with the good (George Michael), the bad (RuPaul, Nik Kershaw) and the bizarre (Leonard Cohen). Of far greater interest was the same year's *Elton John Songbook*, an intriguing collection of Elton covers which included Rod Stewart's 'Country Comfort', Aretha Franklin's 'Border Song', Tom Robinson's 'Elton's Song' and Sandy Denny's 'Candle In The Wind'. The following year, Elton even sanctioned the release of *Reg Dwight's Piano Goes Pop* – a fascinating glimpse of the pre-fame days, which collected together his anonymous imitations of late '60s hits.

The official celebration of Elton and Bernie's work together came in 1991 with *Two Rooms,* a CD, book and TV documentary package featuring more fascinating covers of the much-

loved back catalogue: Kate Bush's trippy 'Rocket Man'; Eric Clapton's powerhouse 'Border Song'; The Beach Boys' chirpy 'Crocodile Rock'; Tina Turner's brazen 'The Bitch Is Back'; and Sinead O'Connor's haunting 'Sacrifice'. The latter's incredulous sleeve note read simply: 'I can't believe no-one did 'Candle In The Wind''.

Two Rooms and *Duets* placed him firmly alongside the new generation of pop acts in the public mind, but Elton had never really been out of touch with the current crop of rock 'n' roll talent. He took a keen interest in nurturing George Michael's solo career, is on nodding terms with Atlanta neighbour Michael Stipe of REM and spoke encouragingly of Take That – praising in particular the songwriting abilities of Gary Barlow, which critics had suggested contained echoes of 1970s classic Elton John. Many pop pickers were sniffy about the success of the Spice Girls, but Elton was a vocal supporter of them too. His gallantry was rewarded by a brief walk-on appearance in 1997's monumentally successful *Spiceworld: The Movie*, and later in the year he returned the compliment in his TV special *An Audience With Elton John*, inviting the girls to join him as special guests on a zesty version of 'Don't Go Breaking My Heart'.

Through all his well-publicised ups and downs, Elton has always remained scrupulously faithful to his music. Despite very real anguish over his addictions, his hair-loss, his sexuality, his marriage and his court battles, he has always kept on recording. The quality may have dipped and soared, but there always remained a deep commitment to the music which had helped the shy, dumpy Reg Dwight escape from Pinner and given Elton John his place on the world stage. 'Some people take three or four years in between each album,' Elton explained to Leslie Bennetts in a 1998 profile for *Vanity Fair*, 'and I think "what are you doing?" The thing that saved my life was that I worked. No matter what shape I was in, I still managed to perform and make records.'

Perhaps it was a spin-off from the personal fulfilment he had found through commitment to his partner David Furnish, but whatever the reason, during the '90s Elton's original material was marked by a new consistency and the best of it achieved a quality the likes of which he hadn't hit in twenty years. For sentimental reasons long-time fans are bound to prefer *Goodbye Yellow Brick Road* or *Don't Shoot Me I'm Only The Piano Player*, simply because the music will always evoke memories of their own younger days. But albums like 1992's *The One*, and particularly 1995's *Made In England*, are exemplary Elton; the latter, besides a biting title track, also included 'Believe' – a power ballad as strong as any the John/Taupin partnership has ever conjured up.

Music still matters to Elton. He studies *Billboard* religiously, and if smugness does emerge in interview, it never concerns the conquering of his addictions or other personal achievements, but always centres on the music: 'I've had a Top 40 single in *Billboard* every year for the last twenty-seven years,' he proudly told *Vanity Fair*, 'I beat Elvis' record. He had twenty-two or twenty-three years.'

Echoes of young Reg's meticulous indexing system can still be found in Elton's collection of CDs, which are kept fastidiously filed, all in strict alphabetical order. And although he has recently passed his first half century, Elton's knowledge of current music remains impressive – clocking the new wave of Britpop bands as well as the latest movements in dance. He is acutely aware of the faintly risible picture of a 50-year-old middle-aged man masquerading as a hip young rock star; however with rock 'n' roll fast approaching its first half century, there

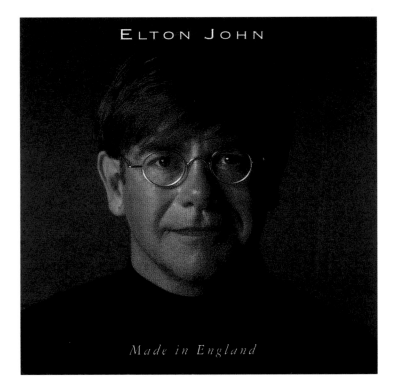

ELTON JOHN

Made in England

is a respect bordering on veneration for acts who have lasted the course. And the '90s Elton accepts that there is no longer any need for those early attention-grabbing antics; the music and performance are enough now to command an audience.

Even if his music no longer makes the mark it did during the 1970s, Elton John can feel proud to be among that select group of musicians who emerged in the late '60s and can still make a living making music. Pop has moved on and the release of an album is no longer the epicentre of many people's lives. Nowadays there are other distractions – the Internet, videos, computers, round-the-clock television. Rock 'n' roll no longer has a monopoly, but its ablest practitioners still command great affection in the hearts of those who grew up with their music. And nowhere is that more evident than in concert.

Touring used to be an expensive but inevitable part of promoting a new album. Now the Rolling Stones, U2, Madonna and REM have upped the ante on the rock 'n' roll tour; and corporate sponsorship, together with money-spinning merchandising opportunities, ensure that even before the band have played a note, they are on the road to profit.

Throughout the early part of 1998, the Elton John and Billy Joel roadshow trundled around the world to the accompaniment of a welter of excited publicity – despite cancellations by Joel owing to illness – selling out massive venues wherever they went, each one seating up to 75,000 eager fans.

The lights dim, and out walks the tiny, dumpy figure. No need now for Donald Duck or Ronald MacDonald costumes – the desire to dress up as Tina Turner, or in the rhinestoned costume of some small South American dictator, has thankfully passed. A full head of expensively acquired hair fringes the discreet designer specs, and the suit is of muted colour and tasteful cut. The exhibitionism has been locked away with the dressing-up box, but this is still a master craftsman at work.

Acknowledging the roar, Elton settles at the piano to present a selection from the new album and then kicks the piano stool away – only metaphorically nowadays – and launches into a staggering and time-consuming trot through the back catalogue. Out come the songs, one after another; hits which peppered the pop landscape of the '70s, material which is part of the emotional baggage of untold hundreds of thousands of people. And as with all the greatest pop music, each time those opening few chords coalesce with the familiar chorus and the half-forgotten lyrical fragments, it seems like the very first time.

It is an astonishing fact that when Elton John first began having hit records, *Ziggy Stardust* was just a twinkle in David Bowie's eye; there was some hope of a Beatles reunion; and still a possibility that Elvis Presley would, one day, perform a concert in Britain. But though times have moved on, this is what Elton John has always done well.

This is the day job. And as he tells those tales again, the audience is with him every step of the way. They have lived their lives to this music and they have read and sympathised as Elton fought his highly-publicised battles. And now he really is the People's Pop Star. In the words of Elton's hero Spike Milligan: 'Which side are you on? – There are no sides, you fool, we're all in this together.' **ej**

A little bit...
Discography

Various CD versions of the early Elton vinyl releases are available. In the

1990s however, the series *Elton John: The Classic Years* saw most of the

albums remastered and re-released, often with bonus tracks. Where available

this improved CD version is listed, together with any extra tracks.

1969
Empty Sky (June)
Empty Sky, Val-Hala, Western Ford Gateway, Hymn 2000, Lady, What's Tomorrow?, Sails, The Scaffold, Skyline Pigeon, Gulliver/Hay Chewed.

Remastered CD (May 1995) + Lady Samantha, All Across the Havens, It's Me That You Need, Just Like Strange Rain.

1970
Elton John (April)
Your Song, I Need You to Turn To, Take Me to the Pilot, No Shoe Strings on Louise, First Episode at Hienton, Sixty Years On, Border Song, The Greatest Discovery, The Cage, The King Must Die.

Remastered CD (May 1995) + Bad Side of the Moon, Grey Seal, Rock 'n' Roll Madonna.

Tumbleweed Connection (October)
Ballad of a Well-Known Gun, Come Down in Time, Country Comfort, Son of Your Father, My Father's Gun, Where to Now St Peter?, Love Song, Amoreena, Talking Old Soldiers, Burn Down the Mission.

Remastered CD (May 1995) + Into the Old Man's Shoes, Madman Across the Water (Original Version).

1971
17.11.70 – The Elton John Live Album (April)
Take Me to the Pilot, Honky Tonk Women, Sixty Years On, Can I Put You On?, Bad Side of the Moon, Medley: Burn Down the Mission/My Baby Left Me/Get Back.

Remastered CD (October 1995) + Amoreena.

Friends (Original Soundtrack Recording) (April)
Friends, Honey Roll, *Variations on Friends Theme (The First Kiss), Seasons, *Variations on Michelle's Song (A Day in the Country), Can I Put You On?, Michelle's Song, *I Meant to Do My Work Today, *Four Moods, Seasons (Reprise).
*These tracks not performed by Elton John

Available on CD as part of the *Elton John - Rare Masters* box set listed below.

Madman Across The Water (November)
Tiny Dancer, Levon, Razor Face, Madman Across the Water, Indian Sunset, Holiday Inn, Rotten Peaches, All the Nasties, Goodbye.

Remastered CD (July 1995) – no bonus tracks.

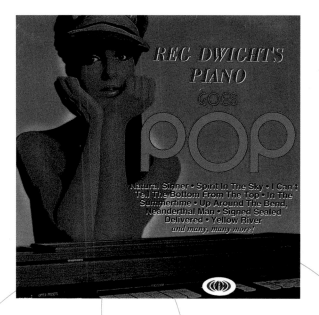

1972
Honky Chateau (May)
Honky Cat, Mellow, I Think I'm Going To Kill Myself, Susie (Dramas), Rocket Man (I Think It's Going to Be a Long, Long Time), Salvation, Slave, Amy, Mona Lisas and Mad Hatters, Hercules.

Remastered CD (July 1995) + Slave (Alt. Version).

1973
Don't Shoot Me I'm only The Piano Player (February)
Daniel, Teacher I Need You, Elderberry Wine, Blues For My Baby and Me, Midnight Creeper, Have Mercy on the Criminal, I'm Gonna Be a Teenage Idol, Texan Love Song, Crocodile Rock, High-Flying Bird.

Remastered CD (May 1995) + Screw You (Young Man's Blues), Jack Rabbit, Whenever You're Ready (We'll Go Steady Again), Skyline Pigeon (Piano Version).

Goodbye Yellow Brick Road (October)
Medley: Funeral For a Friend/Love Lies Bleeding, Candle in the Wind, Bennie and The Jets, Goodbye Yellow Brick Road, This Song Has No Title, Grey Seal, Jamaica Jerk-Off, I've Seen That Movie Too, Sweet Painted Lady, The Ballad of Danny Bailey (1909-34), Dirty Little Girl, All the Girls Love Alice, Your Sister Can't Twist (But She Can Rock 'n' Roll), Saturday Night's Alright for Fighting, Roy Rogers, Social Disease, Harmony.

Remastered CD (May 1995) – no bonus tracks.

1974
Caribou (July)
The Bitch is Back, Pinky, Grimsby, Dixie Lily, Solar Prestige A Gammon, You're So Static, I've Seen the Saucers, Stinker, Don't Let the Sun Go Down On Me, Ticking.

Remastered CD (May 1995) + Pinball Wizard, Sick City, Cold Highway, Step Into Christmas.

1975
Captain Fantastic And The Brown Dirt Cowboy (May)
Captain Fantastic And The Brown Dirt Cowboy, Tower of Babel, Bitter Fingers, Tell Me When the Whistle Blows, Someone Saved My Life Tonight, (Gotta Get a) Meal Ticket, Better Off Dead, Writing, We All Fall in Love Sometimes/Curtains.

Remastered CD (July 1995) + Lucy in the Sky with Diamonds, One Day At A Time, Philadelphia Freedom.

Rock Of The Westies (October)
Medley: Yell Help/Wednesday Night/Ugly, Dan Dare (Pilot of the Future), Island Girl, Grow Some Funk of Your Own, I Feel Like a Bullet (In the Gun of Robert Ford), Street Kids, Hard Luck Story, Feed Me, Billy Bones and The White Bird.

Remastered CD (July 1995) + Don't Go Breaking My Heart.

1976
Here And There (May)
Live album recorded at The Royal Festival Hall and Madison Square Gardens in 1974
Skyline Pigeon, Border Song, Honky Cat, Love Song, Crocodile Rock, Funeral For a Friend/Love Lies Bleeding, Rocket Man (I Think It's Going to Be a Long, Long Time), Bennie and The Jets, Take Me to the Pilot.

Remastered CD (October 1995) expanded into double CD + Take Me To The Pilot (alt version), Country Comfort, Bad Side of the Moon, Burn Down the Mission, Candle in the Wind, Your Song, Saturday Night's Alright for Fighting, Grey Seal, Daniel, You're So Static, Whatever Gets You Thru the Night, Lucy in the Sky with Diamonds, I Saw Her Standing There, Don't Let the Sun Go Down on Me, Your Song, The Bitch is Back.

Blue Moves (October)
Your Starter For…, Tonight, One Horse Town, Chameleon, Boogie Pilgrim, Cage the Songbird, Crazy Water, Shoulder Holster, Sorry Seems to Be the Hardest Word, Out of the Blue, Between Seventeen and Twenty, The Wide-Eyed and Laughing, Someone's Final Song, Where's the Shoorah, If There's a God in Heaven (What's He Waiting For?), Idol, Theme From a Non-Existent TV Series, Bite Your Lip (Get Up and Dance).

Remastered CD (June 1996) – no bonus tracks.

1978
A Single Man (October)
Shine On Through, Return to Paradise, I Don't Care, Big Dipper, It Ain't Gonna Be Easy, Part-Time Love, Georgia, Shooting Star, Madness, Reverie, Song for Guy.

Remastered CD (June 1998) + Ego, Flintstone Boy, I Cry at Night, Lovesick, Strangers.

1979
Victim Of Love (October)
Johnny B. Goode, Warm Love in a Cold World, Born Bad, Thunder in the Night, Spotlight, Street Boogie, Victim of Love.

1980
21 At 33 (May)
Chasing the Crown, Little Jeannie, Sartorial Eloquence, Two Rooms at the End of the World, White Lady White Powder, Dear God, Never Gonna Fall in Love Again, Take Me Back, Give Me the Love.

1981
The Fox (May)
Breaking Down the Barriers, Heart in the Right Place, Just Like Belgium, Nobody Wins, Fascist Faces, Medley: Carla/Etude/Fanfare/Chloe, Heels of the Wind, Elton's Song, The Fox.

1982
Jump Up! (April)
Dear John, Spiteful Child, Ball & Chain, Legal Boys, I Am Your Robot, Blue Eyes, Empty Garden (Hey Hey Johnny), Princess, Where Have All The Good Times Gone?, All Quiet on the Western Front.

1983
Too Low For Zero (June)
Cold as Christmas (In The Middle Of The Year), I'm Still Standing, Too Low For Zero, Religion, I Guess That's Why They Call it the Blues, Crystal, Kiss the Bride, Whipping Boy, My Baby's a Saint, One More Arrow.

Remastered CD (June 1998) + Earn While You Learn, Dreamboat, The Retreat.

1984
Breaking Hearts (June)
Restless, Slow Down Georgie (She's Poison), Who Wears These Shoes?, Breaking Hearts (Ain't What It Used To Be), Li'l 'Frigerator, Passengers, In Neon, Burning Buildings, Did He Shoot Her?, Sad Songs (Say So Much).

1985
Ice On Fire (November)
This Town, Cry to Heaven, Soul Glove, Nikita, Too Young, Wrap Her Up, Satellite, Tell Me What the Papers Say, Candy by the Pound, Shoot Down the Moon.

Remastered CD (June 1998) + The Man Who Never Died, Restless (live), Sorry Seems to Be the Hardest Word (live), I'm Still Standing (live).

1986
Leather Jackets (November)
Leather Jackets, Hoop of Fire, Don't Trust That Woman, Go It Alone, Gypsy Heart, Slow Rivers, Heartache All Over the World, Angeline, Memory of Love, Paris, I Fall Apart.

1987
Live In Australia With The Melbourne Symphony Orchestra (September)
Sixty Years On, I Need You To Turn To, The Greatest Discovery, Tonight, Sorry Seems to Be the Hardest Word, The King Must Die, Take Me to the Pilot, Tiny Dancer, Have Mercy on the Criminal, Madman Across the Water, Candle in the Wind, Burn Down the Mission, Your Song, Don't Let the Sun Go Down on Me.

Remastered CD (June 1998) – no bonus tracks.

1988
Reg Strikes Back (July)
Town of Plenty, A Word in Spanish, Mona Lisas and Mad Hatters (Part 2), I Don't Wanna Go On with You Like That, Japanese Hands, Goodbye Marlon Brando, The Camera Never Lies, Heavy Traffic, Poor Cow, Since God Invented Girls.

Remastered CD (June 1998) + Rope Around a Fool, I Don't Wanna Go On with You Like That (2 mixes), Mona Lisas and Mad Hatters (Part 2 – different mix).

1989
Sleeping With The Past (September)
Durban Deep, Healing Hands, Whispers, Club at the End of the Street, Sleeping with the Past, Stone's Throw from Hurtin', Sacrifice, I Never Knew Her Name, Amazes Me, Blue Avenue.

Remastered CD (June 1998) + Dancing in the End Zone, Love is a Cannibal.

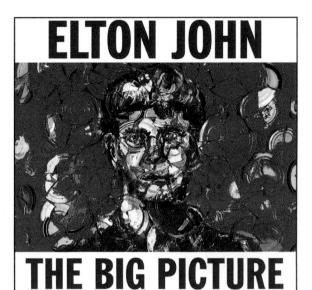

1992
The One (June)
Simple Life, The One, Sweat It Out, Runaway Train, Whitewash County, The North, When a Woman Doesn't Want You, Emily, On Dark Street, Understanding Women, The Last Song.

Remastered CD (June 1998) + Suit of Wolves, Fat Boys and Ugly Girls.

1993
Duets (November)
Teardrops (k.d.lang), When I Think About Love (I Think About You) (P.M.Dawn), The Power (Little Richard), Shakey Ground (Don Henley), True Love (Kiki Dee), If You Were Me (Chris Rea), A Woman's Needs (Tammy Wynette), Old Friend (Nik Kershaw), Go On and On (Gladys Knight), Don't Go Breaking My Heart (RuPaul), Ain't Nothing Like the Real Thing (Marcella Detroit), I'm Your Puppet (Paul Young), Love Letters (Bonnie Raitt), Born to Lose (Leonard Cohen), Don't Let the Sun Go Down on Me (George Michael), Duets for One (solo).

1994
The Lion King (October – with Tim Rice & Hans Zimmer)
Circle Of Life, I Just Can't Wait To Be King, Be Prepared, Hakuna Matata, Can You Feel The Love Tonight, This Land, …To Die For, Under The Stars, King Of Pride Rock, Circle Of Life, I Just Can't Wait To Be King, Can You Feel The Love Tonight.

1995
Made In England (March)
Believe, Made in England, House, Cold, Pain, Belfast, Latitude, Please, Man, Lies, Blessed.

Love Songs (November)
Sacrifice, Candle in the Wind, I Guess That's Why They Call it The Blues, Don't Let the Sun Go Down on Me (duet with George Michael), Sorry Seems to Be the Hardest Word, Blue Eyes, Daniel, Nikita, Your Song, The One, Someone Saved My Life Tonight, True Love, Can You Feel the Love Tonight, Circle of Life, Blessed, Please, Song for Guy.

1997
The Big Picture (September)
Long Way From Happiness, Live Like Horses, The End Will Come, If the River Can Bend, Love's Got a Lot to Answer For, Something About The Way You Look Tonight, The Big Picture, Recover Your Soul, January, I Can't Steer My Heart Clear of You, Wicked Dreams.

TRIBUTE ALBUMS
Two Rooms – Celebrating The Songs Of Elton John & Bernie Taupin (October 1991)
Border Song (Eric Clapton), Rocket Man (Kate Bush), Come Down In Time (Sting), Saturday Night's Alright for Fighting (The Who), Crocodile Rock (The Beach Boys), Daniel (Wilson Phillips), Sorry Seems to Be the Hardest Word (Joe Cocker), Levon (Jon Bon Jovi), The Bitch is Back (Tina Turner), Philadelphia Freedom (Daryl Hall & John Oates), Your Song (Rod Stewart), Don't Let The Sun Go Down on Me (Oleta Adams), Madman Across the Water (Bruce Hornsby), Sacrifice (Sinead O'Connor), Burn Down the Mission (Phil Collins), Tonight (George Michael).

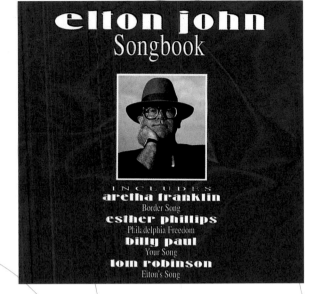

Elton John Songbook
(September 1993)

Hey Lord You Made the Night Too Long (John Baldry), Breakdown Blues (Bread and Beer Band), Turn to Me (Plastic Penny), Country Comfort (Rod Stewart), Border Song (Aretha Franklin), 71-75 New Oxford Street (Mr Bloe), Let Me Be Your Car (Rod Stewart), Don't Let the Sun Go Down on Me (The Three Degrees), Planes (Colin Blunstone), Candle in the Wind (Sandy Denny), Your Song (Billy Paul), Philadelphia Freedom (Esther Phillips), Strangers (Randy Meisner), Sweet Heart on Parade (Judy Collins), Sorry Seems to Be the Hardest Word (Elaine Paige), The Rumour (Olivia Newton-John), Sacrifice (Brenda Cochrane), Someone Saved My Life Tonight (Walter Jackson), Elton's Song (Tom Robinson).

COMPILATIONS
The Very Best Of Elton John
(November 1990)

Your Song, Rocket Man (I Think It's Going to Be a Long Long Time), Honky Cat, Crocodile Rock, Daniel, Goodbye Yellow Brick Road, Saturday Night's Alright for Fighting, Candle in the Wind, Don't Let the Sun Go Down on Me, Lucy in the Sky with Diamonds, Philadelphia Freedom, Someone Saved My Life Tonight, Pinball Wizard, The Bitch is Back, Don't Go Breaking My Heart, Bennie and The Jets, Sorry Seems to Be the Hardest Word, Song For Guy, Part Time Love, Blue Eyes, I Guess That's Why They Call It The Blues, I'm Still Standing, Kiss the Bride, Sad Songs, Passengers, Nikita, I Don't Wanna Go On With You Like That, Sacrifice, Easier to Walk Away, You Gotta Love Someone.

There have been a number of compilations over the years, but this two CD package is the best released over the '90s.

BOX SETS
To Be Continued . . .
(October 1990 – since deleted)

A four CD box-set including rare singles, demo versions and live tracks.

Elton John – Rare Masters
(January 1993)

This two CD package included, for the first time on CD, the entire soundtrack of *Friends*, as well a collection of B-sides, rarities and hard-to-get singles. In his revealing liner notes, Bernie Taupin describes the songs here as "the ones that got away".

MISCELLANEOUS
Reg Dwight's Piano Goes Pop
(November 1994)

My Baby Loves Lovin', Cottonfields, Lady D'Arbanville, Natural Sinner, United We Stand, Spirit in the Sky, Travellin' Band, I Can't Tell the Bottom From the Top, Good Morning Freedom, Young, Gifted and Black, In the Summertime, Up Around the Bend, Snake in the Grass, Neanderthal Man, She Sold Me Magic, Come and Get It, Love of the Common People, Signed Sealed Delivered, It's All in the Game, Yellow River.

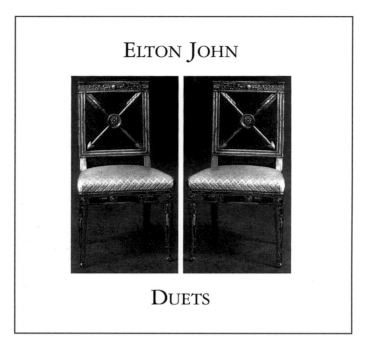

ELTON JOHN

DUETS

BIBLIOGRAPHY

First off, Philip Norman's exhaustive 500-page biography
Elton (Hutchinson, 1991) does its subject full justice, memorably
complementing Norman's Beatles and Rolling Stones biographies.
Other books consulted during the writing of this book include:

Off The Record: An Oral History Of Popular Music
Joe Smith
(Sidgwick & Jackson, 1989)

Two Rooms: Elton John & Bernie Taupin In Their Own Words
(Boxtree, 1991)

Elton John: A Visual Documentary
Nigel Goodall
(Omnibus, 1993)

Elton John & Bernie Taupin: The Complete Lyrics
(Pavilion, 1994)

Meaty Beaty Big & Bouncy
Edited by Dylan Jones
(Hodder & Stoughton, 1996)

Elton John's Flower Fantasies
Caroline Cass
(Weidenfeld & Nicholson, 1997)

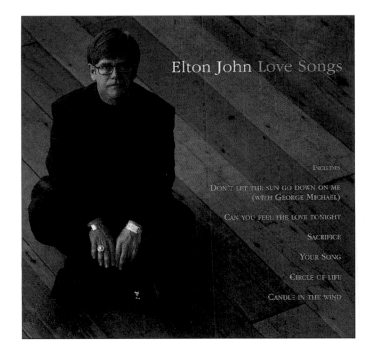

PICTURE CREDITS

The author and publishers have made every reasonable effort to contact all copyright holders. Any errors that may have occurred are inadvertent and anyone who for any reason has not been contacted is invited to write to the publishers so that a full acknowledgement may be made in subsequent editions of this work.